T0327208

BANKING FOR A BETTER WORLD

To our children, their children and their children's children

BANKING FOR A BETTER WORLD

NANNO KLEITERP
IN CONVERSATION WITH
MARIJN WIERSMA

AUP

The publication of this book is made possible through the support of FMO. The proceeds of this book will go to "Stand for trees" for the "Cordillera Azul National Park" in Peru.

Cover design & lay-out: WAT ontwerpers

Amsterdam University Press English-language titles are distributed in the US and Canada by the University of Chicago Press.

ISBN 978 94 6298 351 9
e-ISBN 978 90 4853 380 0 (pdf)
NUR 781

© FMO / Amsterdam University Press B.V., Amsterdam 2017

CONTENTS

7   Foreword

9   Introduction

11   The Defining Moments of My Working Life

19   Ensuring the Well-Being of Both a Growing Population
     and Our Planet

45   Sustainable Development as a Business Opportunity

61   Financing Sustainable Development

77   The Role of Development Banks

105   New Business Models for Sustainable Development

125   FMO's Transition to Sustainable Development

139   Epilogue

141   Acknowledgements

143   Acronym Glossary

145   References

FOREWORD

*This book is about banking for a better world. "Banking" and
"a better world" are not often associated with one another,
and yet this book argues that the latter will require the former.
In examining the challenges the world currently faces in reducing
poverty and inequality, addressing climate change, and
safeguarding biodiversity, this book highlights the changing
responsibilities of businesses, governments, financial institutions,
and civil society. It also details the crucial role that development
banks can play as catalysts for sustainable development.*

A series of conferences that took place in 2015 have led to nothing short
of a paradigm shift in the way we think about international development,
the environment, and finance. They have transformed the division of roles
between North and South and between governments and the private
sector. This shift has opened up tremendous opportunities for businesses,
banks, civil society, knowledge organisations, and governments alike to
contribute to achieving a sustainable world – one in which more than nine
billion people (the expected world population in 2050) live well and
within the planet's ecological limits. *Banking for a Better World* asserts that
sustainable development is not only doable but also desirable for all.
Development banks will be essential in bringing about the much-needed
scaling up of sustainability projects by serving as important bridges
between the public and private sectors, thereby maximising the impact of
the scarce government resources currently available.

Banking for a Better World is based on a series of conversations that took
place over the last eight years between myself, Chief Executive Officer of
FMO, and Marijn Wiersma, who has been enabling innovation and
change at FMO. These conversations delved into such topics as FMO's

role in the path to sustainable development, the role of the public and private sectors in the same path, the development of innovative business models, and how to remain relevant in a rapidly changing world.

The stories in this book are based on my 40 years of experience in developing countries, of which the last 29 have been in various roles at FMO. I saw my departure from FMO as an excellent opportunity to condense my experience into something that could be shared and, we hope, something from which to learn. I knew that the best way to transform my ideas into meaningful stories was to base them on the conversations I have had with Marijn over the years. Without this cooperation, this book would not have seen the light of day. Although the book is inspired by our conversations, it is not written in the form of a conversation.

INTRODUCTION

This book can be seen as a kind of journey – a journey into my thoughts and experiences as a person who has been involved with developing countries for 40 years. It begins with some of the defining moments of my life, moments that have been crucial to the choices I have made in my work and that together form the basis of my convictions concerning international development.

Chapter two addresses several worldwide issues the global community faces today, including climate change and its adverse effects, the steady increase in inequality, and unsustainable taxation and business practices. These are all issues that stand in the way of what I consider the ultimate global challenge: ensuring the well-being of both a growing population and our increasingly fragile planet. I then address what I believe to be a paradigm shift that was triggered by three very important conferences that took place in 2015: the Addis Ababa conference on Financing for Development, the United Nations Sustainable Development Summit, and the Paris conference on climate change. I conclude the chapter by defining the roles that should be played by the most important players in the field of development: governments, businesses, civil society (including non-governmental organisations), and financial institutions.

In the third chapter, I consider the role of business in helping the world achieve sustainable development. It is clear that the relationship between business, banking, and society is evolving. Businesses and banks are increasingly finding themselves challenged by consumers and the society at large to make genuine and tangible contributions to a better world. For their part, governments need to accelerate the pace of this change through their policies and frameworks. Civil society can also help set the tempo by mobilising sustainable consumer demand and by challenging the status quo. Finally, businesses must incorporate sustainability into the core of their operations.

Chapter four discusses the role of the financial sector in making sustainable development bankable on a large scale. The annual gap in the amount of investment needed to achieve the Global Goals is currently estimated to be US $2 trillion, making it essential for the financial sector to accelerate and scale up its involvement. However, scaling is only possible when financial institutions, the private sector, and governments collaborate as partners.

Chapter five explains the role that development banks can play in financing green and inclusive growth. I demonstrate how development banks can build bridges between financial players with different risk appetites by catalysing investment, mobilising their own network, and providing scalable examples of successful financing of sustainable development. I end the chapter with examples in which development banks have been game changers in a number of sectors in Africa, South America, and Asia.

Chapter six builds on the previous chapter by highlighting several impressive examples in such fields as environmental finance and inclusive finance. While not widely known, there is a considerable amount of inspiring work taking place and new business models are emerging in the developing world, all of which are currently being financed mainly by development banks and foundations. This needs to be scaled up by involving the private sector on a much larger scale in the financing and implementation of sustainable development projects. Incidentally, I do not wish to pretend that the examples I use in this book are the best or the only examples out there. They are simply the ones that I have firsthand knowledge of.

In the final chapter, I offer some insights into how FMO has navigated and adapted to the shifting global landscape during my time as CEO. I wrap up the book by acknowledging and thanking the many people involved in this project for their invaluable contributions.

THE DEFINING MOMENTS OF MY WORKING LIFE

On a sunny day in September 2013, my daughter and I were enjoying a ferry ride back to the Dutch mainland, not far from where the dikes hold back the North Sea. We had just attended a three-day sustainability forum on the island of Terschelling, and our heads were buzzing with ideas. The conference had provided eye-openers on climate change, tipping points, and biodiversity for us to mull over and consider. It was clear that the international discussion on the ingredients of our collective future was taking shape. The new perspectives we had heard were enlightening but also at times alarming.

A SENSE OF URGENCY

It was the first time I had taken my daughter – who was 30 at the time – to this annual conference, and I was eager to hear her thoughts. What sort of conclusions had she reached? What insights had this weekend revealed for her future? It was my sincere hope that this experience had highlighted for her many issues that were close to my heart, so I awaited her answer eagerly. She thought for some time, weighing her words. Finally, she turned to me and put it flatly: "Dad, looking at all these problems, I don't think I want to have kids." I was shocked. She continued: there had been a lot of talk, but what concrete steps were we making to plot an alternative course? What *was* the alternative course? For her, the urgency of the discussion rang hollow. It was clear that there were plenty of people at least willing to discuss the situation, but the actual change achieved so far – the execution itself – was too minimal and occurred too infrequently to convince her that enough would happen in time for the next generation. It was at that moment that I realised yet again that we needed more action and we needed it fast.

As the CEO of one of the largest bilateral development banks in the world, I was in a position to bring together the necessary partners and help catalyse the funding needed for a sustainable world, a better world. My daughter made me feel once more the sense of urgency to act and make sustainable development happen. In order to stay relevant in a rapidly changing world, we need to ask ourselves as citizens, as businessmen and women, as bankers, as civil servants: what do I see as a better world? And how can I contribute to achieving this? Our answers will, after all, determine what our future will look like.

This moment with my daughter came at a point in time when I thought that I had been on the right track with FMO. We had done everything within our mandate to help build sustainable societies. However, my daughter made it clear that it was still not enough.

Before becoming the CEO of FMO, I had had a number of such defining moments. If I look back at my job interview in 1987 with the general manager of FMO, I remember asking him what the career opportunities were. His response was: "The sky's the limit. Anyone can become CEO." I was thirty-four years old at the time. I had assumed that I would work at FMO for a few years before returning to Latin America where I had worked for the last ten. I was certainly not going to stay more than three years – at most, five. Twenty-nine years later, I am still here, but there is no doubt that a lot has happened at FMO since.

In the first year of my economics degree, I remember having frequent discussions with my fellow students on whether profit maximisation was really what motivated all human behaviour. Even at that stage I had my doubts, and it was for this reason that I ended up at an organisation that sets a profit target but only as a precondition to maximising its social and environmental impact. After obtaining my Bachelor's degree, I chose to study sociological economics for my Master's. While the discipline no longer exists, the choice reflected my conviction that an economic model is of no use if it fails to reflect societal and human behaviour. These studies aligned seamlessly with my work at FMO in the years that followed.

AN EQUAL FOOTING

FMO's business-to-business approach appeals to me because it involves working with people on an equal footing. We provide the finance, and the client knows that it must pay interest (or a dividend) on its loan (or investment). No hidden strings, no ulterior motives. My experience over the years has shown me that that is a better way of facilitating sustainable development in the private sector than providing grants, as is the case with development aid. When money is being offered for free, people are willing to promise almost anything to receive it. There is no equal footing in such a relationship.

Let me explain where this conviction of mine came from. Between 1978 and 1980, I worked in Peru on a rural development project funded by a Dutch government grant. The grant had been given to the Peruvian government with the intention of supporting small farmers, which was in line with the Dutch government's policies on international development. As part of the grant, the Netherlands provided tractors, cars, and training for agricultural engineers. These were all accepted by the Peruvian government, whose real intention was to support medium-sized farmers because of the much bigger impact they had on agricultural production and thus economic growth. The result? Constant tension and conflict in the project execution as the Dutch project developers attempted to support the small farmers while their Peruvian counterparts tried to redirect as many resources as possible to the medium-sized farmers.

As my wife comes from that region in Peru, I have had the opportunity to observe the progress of that project during my yearly visits to the region. What I saw after many years was that the only real impact the project achieved was a dozen well-trained engineers who have since become leaders in local institutions. One even became a successful president of the region. That was the positive side, but in my eyes, one of the main reasons the project failed to reach its objectives was the misalignment between donor and recipient objectives. That difference could only arise because, financially speaking, both parties had nothing to lose. When a project involves a development bank and a company, however, the failure of the project means a real financial loss for both, which significantly reduces the likelihood of a misalignment of objectives.

MARKET MECHANISMS

I am convinced that the best way to contribute to sustainable development is through the private sector. I developed this conviction in the 1980s when I worked for the Nicaraguan Investment Fund and the Ministry of Planning during the Sandinista regime. It was a fascinating and inspiring time, and one that dispelled a number of illusions for me.

At that time, I believed that society was "constructible" and that that was the road to a just society. The Sandinista regime in Nicaragua ignored market forces. Because the people in the cities needed cheap food, food prices were capped, which then created a food shortage because farmers could no longer earn enough to make a living. Black markets full of contraband began to emerge. The number of cattle in the country dropped by 50% because farmers took them to neighbouring countries.

At the Nicaraguan development bank, I remember completing a due diligence on a palm oil project and concluding that it was loss-making. We then introduced a 'special' exchange rate for palm oil to make investments in palm oil attractive. This was an easy fix with dangerous results: a distorted market and higher inflation.

My experience in Nicaragua made me realise that while capitalism is a system full of problems, it is at present the best system we have if it is made sustainable, albeit one that necessitates policies for curbing market excesses. From then on, I was convinced that in order to build a better world, market mechanisms, the private sector, and entrepreneurs had to work alongside governments, which should facilitate business while guarding against market excesses.

MY EXPERIENCE LEADING FMO

I had the luxury of knowing one year in advance that I would become CEO of FMO. This gave me time to prepare myself for this challenging position. I knew that I wanted to take some kind of management course, maybe at Harvard or MIT. In the end, I chose the Comenius Leadership Programme which offered me the opportunity to attend lectures at seven top European universities for three days at a time every two months. What made the Comenius Programme so special was my fifteen fellow 'students', who were all in leadership positions. The bonding we experienced went so deep that, since completing the programme, we still meet twice a year.

The programme's number one rule was that you may only ask questions with the purpose of gaining a deeper understanding. We were requested to withhold our opinions. I have tried to keep that as a core principle whenever I talk with someone in my leadership capacity. Another lesson that stuck with me was 'doing by not doing', a Taoist precept that was explained to us in a lecture by Patricia de Marteleare, a Flemish philosopher and author. Afterwards, I recalled that a good friend had given me the book *The Tao of Leadership*. I have used the book to discuss management principles with my management teams several times. There were also lectures on Chinese medicine, ethics, and how legal systems evolve – all mind-expanding experiences.

I also took a sabbatical for eight weeks to allow myself some distance and some time for introspection. The best advice I received on what to do during my sabbatical was to focus on a specific theme – something other than development banking. As I am someone who finds it easiest to deal with facts, I chose to focus on a subject I knew almost nothing about: spirituality. With a stack of books by the Dalai Lama, Martin Buber, and other spiritual leaders, I set out with my wife to connect with the world outside of banking and to try new things. Though I am not religious, I found myself taking the time to listen to a sermon while traveling through Spain, observing how others connected and what it meant to them. This was a new world to me, one in which the unexplainable was commonplace. I was reading a book about near-death experiences while we travelled to Peru to visit my mother-in-law who was dying. I found myself almost laughed at by my wife's family in Peru because to them it was funny that a book had been written about such obvious things. Ultimately, this period was a time of both introspection and observation, a time to reassess what I believed in the context of my upcoming role. It made me realise that there was more between heaven and earth than I could observe, and it reminded me to take the time to listen to others and to be open to what I could not immediately understand. Thinking about what I should do and give as CEO, I managed to find peace by accepting who I am and trusting that that is the only thing I can give. I think you need to reach a certain age to accept that.

I have always felt grateful for the chance to work at and eventually lead a bank whose purpose is none other than to create a better world. FMO is a company with a clear commitment to integrity and social responsibility. I am grateful for having had the opportunity to influence that direction. While attaining such a leadership position is something I have aspired to, it was not something I would have called a perfect match. I had my doubts before taking on the position. For someone who does not enjoy celebrating his own birthday – to be the centre of all that attention – I stepped into a role where I was more or less the centre of attention every single day.

Being the CEO of FMO has been both special and rewarding. People expect you to have an opinion on all kinds of world problems, and they listen. Though I am not someone who has an instant opinion on every subject, it has been fascinating to study all the ins and outs of various issues and to develop an informed opinion. As CEO, I had the honour of being invited to meetings and events that a 'normal' person would never attend. I remember going to dinners for foreign heads of state hosted by the Dutch King and Queen as well as lectures at the Amsterdam palace where insightful and inspirational figures spoke about current issues. A few years ago, the subject was the financial crisis and what would happen next. One of the speakers was Lamido Sanusi Sanusi, the president of the Nigerian central bank – an impressive man. The title of his speech was *What Can Europe Learn from Africa?* To me, it was a clear sign of the direction in which international relations was moving.

Before the financial crisis, no one could have imagined an African central banker lecturing the Dutch financial sector on what it could learn from him. His main argument was that central banks in Europe should do the same as he had done in Nigeria, namely to apply the rule of law and jail several bank CEOs. He stressed the importance of maintaining much stricter control over nominations to the management and supervisory boards of banks, a provision that was applied a few years later in the Netherlands. To those who argued that a central bank should not assume such a role, his response was: If you don't like it, stop working in the business of safeguarding people's savings and start a grocery store instead.

CONNECTING THE DOTS

I thought it was a good idea to start the first chapter on a personal note so that the reader can situate the rest of the book within this personal context. Looking back now with the wisdom of hindsight, FMO fits almost perfectly with the beliefs I had formed in the years before I started working there. In my conversations with Marijn about my role at the bank, the choices I had made, and the things I did and did not do, it became easier to pinpoint the moments in my life that influenced me most. I could not help but find it curious to discover that, after so many years, there seems to be a consistent line of thinking and decision-making that I was never conscious of until now.

ENSURING THE WELL-BEING OF BOTH A GROWING POPULATION AND OUR PLANET

A few years ago, I visited a fantastic three-day conference entitled How on Earth Can We Live Together? Set in the quiet, beautiful village of Tällberg on the edge of Siljan Lake in the south of Sweden, the conference was held under the high canopy of a circus tent because there was no conference venue that could hold anywhere close to 400 people.

The attendees came from all over the world from the fields of business, science, civil society, and governments and were anywhere between the ages of twenty and seventy. Each of us wore a simple name tag without reference to our organisation, position, or nationality. The only thing we knew of each other was that we all had a connection to sustainability. It was a fascinating and inspiring event for me, and it opened my eyes to the urgency with which we all need to collectively act to address climate change. Beyond climate issues, the world still faces many unanswered challenges without effective solutions, challenges that require new and innovative solutions.

THE TÄLLBERG CONFERENCE

The Tällberg conference was especially engaging because most conferences tend to take place in dark meeting rooms in hotel basements and are attended by people from similar backgrounds who pop in and out of the panels, only to vanish at the end of the day. Not at Tällberg. In a tent with a beautiful view over the lake, together with a richly diverse group of people, I listened to music in between the panels and speeches and went on nature walks during the programme. For me, it was three days of contemplation in a completely different environment, three days of meeting different people over breakfast, lunch, and dinner. Even now, I am still in touch with a dozen people from Tällberg with whom I continue to have inspiring conversations again and again. I met many young people with innovative ideas who had started their own companies, and I was struck by the diversity of subjects covered, ranging from sea life and forests to renewable energy and finance. Tällberg inspired me and has informed FMO's business strategy. Several of the conferences that FMO has organised in recent years have included important elements of Tällberg in them.

With so much inspiration and expertise in one place, I decided to attend the conference the following year.

A CLEAR VISION

It was during my second visit to Tällberg that I came across something that left me astounded. At one presentation, a specialist in visual language from Stanford University stood in front of a huge poster depicting a vision of what businesses needed to do to attain sustainable development, backcasting from 2050 to 2010. As I listened to him explain the different flows and how each connected and built on the other, it quickly became clear to me that this was it! For the first time, I saw how everything could be brought together. I was seeing my belief – the need to attain sustainable development through equitable growth within ecological limits – being translated into concrete steps. When most people discuss global challenges, they tend to describe a messy and tangled web of problems. Addressing one issue always seems to create a problem somewhere else. However, here I was watching someone define exactly what needed to be done. More than an inspiration, it came as a relief: it seems I had finally found a path.

Only later did I find out that what Stanford's Robert Horn had presented at Tällberg was the World Business Council for Sustainable Development's *Vision 2050*. Soon thereafter, I had that poster mounted up on the wall in my office as well as in FMO's restaurant. Every time a guest walked into my office, I would draw his/her attention to the wall and explain the poster and what it entails, just to get people thinking about how business can solve world challenges. This has often proven to be a valuable start to meetings, whether it be with regulators, clients, or government officials.

Vision 2050 starts with a simply stated ambition: to have nine billion people living well, and within the limits of the planet, by 2050. Taking this as the end goal, it concludes that by 2050, we would need to have energy-generating buildings, CO_2-free transport and energy generation, double the productivity in the agricultural sector, zero deforestation and continuous land restoration, the incorporation of the value of nature (externalities) in prices, to name a few examples. These are all simple objectives but not so simple to realise.

The reason I am so keen on *Vision 2050* is that it provides insight into very complex global problems, showing the concrete steps that have to be taken in the next 40 years in order to realise sustainable societies throughout the world. What I especially like about *Vision 2050* is its optimism: the message is that if we simply do what is needed, it is possible to create these sustainable societies. The expected growth in world population means there will be two billion new consumers over the coming forty years – new consumers who will translate into new business. At the same time, we have to completely redesign the way we produce and consume. This is a great chance for businesses because it offers fantastic investment opportunities for innovation and new technologies. Rather than thinking in terms of obstacles, the report prefers to focus on the opportunities, as I tend do.

Pathways towards a Better World, based on "Vision 2050"*

VISION 2050

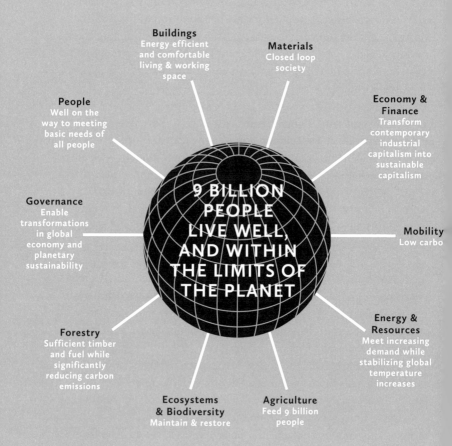

Buildings
Energy efficient and comfortable living & working space

Materials
Closed loop society

People
Well on the way to meeting basic needs of all people

Economy & Finance
Transform contemporary industrial capitalism into sustainable capitalism

Governance
Enable transformations in global economy and planetary sustainability

Mobility
Low carbo

Forestry
Sufficient timber and fuel while significantly reducing carbon emissions

Energy & Resources
Meet increasing demand while stabilizing global temperature increases

Ecosystems & Biodiversity
Maintain & restore

Agriculture
Feed 9 billion people

9 BILLION PEOPLE LIVE WELL, AND WITHIN THE LIMITS OF THE PLANET

* World Business Council for Sustainable Development

Vision 2050 defines the destination we should aim for and how to get there. It also makes it unmistakably clear that we have very little time and an awful lot to do before we get there.

FROM ECONOMIC GROWTH TO A CIRCULAR ECONOMY

An important premise underlying *Vision 2050* is that there will be a shift in the economic balance toward today's emerging markets, where the middle class will swell as a share of the population. The report estimates that these trends – along with the changeover to sustainable development – will open up opportunities for business in the order of US $0.5 to US $1.5 trillion annually, which could rise to US $3 to US $10 trillion by 2050. This has profound implications for business.

People often ask me: "Why are you so convinced that economic growth is necessary?" In the next four decades, the world population is expected to grow from seven to nine billion people – an extra two billion people, all of whom will be moving toward a consumption pattern similar to that of the developed world. My nieces and nephews in Peru have similar desires to my children in the Netherlands: they want to have a smartphone, a laptop, a car, and they want to be able to travel. The list goes on. Just like us, they want to have the things that will make their lives more convenient. This is the case with the rapidly growing middle class in all developing countries. While these are normal desires which they have the right to have, fulfilling these desires would require a substantial increase in the amount of energy and resources used and in the infrastructure that will need to be built. Given that the resources on our planet are finite, it is impossible for the world to continue accelerating on a linear path of economic growth. The World Business Council for Sustainable Development estimates that, at today's rates of consumption, in 2050 we would need the equivalent of 2.3 planets to sustain our population's growth. Assuming that we will not have found new planets to inhabit by then, we will have to make radical changes in order to solve our problems. We need zero or low-carbon economic growth that is equitable at the same time. We need to move towards a circular economy. We need to restore our forests and the biodiversity of our planet. These are not "nice-to-haves"; they are indispensable for our collective well-being on a single planet in the near future.

I firmly believe it is the developed world's responsibility to shrink its footprint as quickly as possible to create space for the needs of emerging countries. Since the Industrial Revolution, developed countries have used up more than their fair share of the carbon dioxide budget worldwide. We in the developed world have had the luxury of being able to make environmental mistakes, but those days are now over. While it is true that developing countries may be able to leapfrog steps and use new technologies to jump directly into a circular economy with low-carbon economic growth, this does not absolve the developed countries from their responsibilities. The world must shift its focus away from linear models of economic growth. For their part, developed economies should start to apply themselves to the redistribution of labour and wealth for the purpose of creating sustainable societies.

WORLDWIDE ISSUES

I cannot emphasise enough the incredible progress the world has made in reducing poverty. Only 25 years ago, some 40% of the world population lived below the poverty line. Since then, that percentage has dropped to less than 10% of the world population – even as the world population increased by almost three billion people over the same period! And yet strangely enough, the general perception is that we have achieved little in the fight against poverty. Nothing could be further from the truth.

POVERTY IS REDUCED ...

If we look at how and where this decline in poverty occurred, the big driver has been – and still is – China. In the last 30 years, the share of those living below the poverty line in China has decreased from 84% to just 12% of its population. This impressive feat was made possible by China's economic miracle: its economy has grown on average by almost 10% per year for the last 25 years. The Chinese economy is now 20 times larger than it was a quarter of a century ago. This is proof that economic growth is an important driver in reducing poverty. Chinese economic growth has provided an enormous impetus to many developing countries, and it has allowed a number of emerging markets to enjoy a period of boom from 1990 to 2015, albeit with crises and hiccups along the way for some. India has also made impressive progress in reducing poverty: it has halved its poverty rate to 33% in the last 20 years. The share of the poor in Latin America's population likewise dropped, from 12% to 6%. The one region that has struggled to reduce poverty despite experiencing economic growth was Sub-Saharan Africa.

It used to be that you could divide the world neatly into where the haves and the have-nots lived. In 1990, 90% of those subsisting below the poverty line lived in low-income countries, but today only 20% of the world's poor can be found in such countries. From the point of view of the developed world, this raises an important question: are we still needed to solve the problems of these countries, which have now joined the ranks of middle-income countries? Are we morally obliged to do so? If we look at the statistics, the developed world appears to have already given its answer: the percentage of official development funding going to these middle-income countries has been steadily decreasing. Although more poor people now live in countries whose governments have the resources to help them, the world still faces the unacceptable fact that 700 million people are living below the international poverty line of US $1.90 a day. Development must shift its focus and strategies to address their needs. If we invest in poor people rather than poor countries in a way that addresses both the environment and national growth, this would go a long way towards achieving stability in many parts of the world.

... BUT INEQUALITY INCREASES ...

The logical consequence of a reduction in poverty is a growing middle class – something I believe is essential for political stability. There is, however, another global trend that is threatening to undermine this increase in stability, and that is that the rich are becoming richer much faster than the poor. The richest 1% of people on this planet now have the same amount of wealth as the rest of the world combined. It is alarming – and unjustifiable – that the richest 1% possess 50% of the world's financial wealth.

Income inequality is thus increasing: the poor are becoming less poor at a relatively slower rate. Why should this be considered a problem? Shouldn't we simply be focused on reducing poverty? Certainly, tackling poverty should remain our first concern, but in my opinion, the problem with income inequality is that it excludes a significant portion of the world population from the benefits of economic development.

The exclusion of certain groups within society – women, youth, indigenous populations, and subsistence farmers, for example – occurs for a number of reasons rooted in political, social, technological, geographic, environmental, and economic circumstances. These 'excluded' groups lack access to basic services such as healthcare, education, clean drinking water, and sanitary services. And because these group have no access to the financial services needed to kick-start their economic empowerment, they are at risk of being left behind in any national upswing. To illustrate, allow me to share the story of an Indian family I visited.

In 2014, I went to visit a small village outside of Calcutta, India. Together with one of our clients, an Indian microfinance bank, I went to talk to a family that had obtained microloans in order to set up a mom-and-pop shop and secure a piece of land to raise a few cows and chickens and to harvest vegetables. In a village without electricity, running water, or any other basic amenities, this family warmly opened up their home to me. Over a generous, home-cooked meal we discussed their dreams or rather their single "ambitious" aspiration: to offer their three children a brighter future. These parents wanted nothing more than for their children to lead a better, safer life than they were now living. They understood that in order to achieve that, their children needed to have access to an education, better health services, and necessary credit.

Sheltered from the Indian heat, we sat on the floor where the rich smell of the soil mixed with the herbs as we spoke. The mother's eyes danced with light as she shared their story. This family was doing okay at that moment in time, but therein lay the crux of the problem. Poverty for them was not about hunger; it is not about having absolutely nothing. The issue is that the poor have no safety net. They live with the constant fear that their livelihood will be destroyed from one moment to the next. This uncertainty is what makes the poor so vulnerable. This family had lost everything – including their previous loan – in a flood. They were victims of the vicissitudes of their environment. What made it difficult for them to pick themselves up and start over again was their lack of access to the tools needed to move on, but somehow they had managed to do so.

It became painfully clear in this case that development finance could and should do more; that everyone – both in the public and private spheres – had the means to do more; and that we were collectively failing this family with our inaction. By creating new and innovative financial solutions – solutions that present the right players with the right tools – sustainable development finance could provide my host family with the access to healthcare, education, and the energy supply they needed to break out of poverty once and for all. Micro-financing could provide these people with temporary relief perhaps, but it was not a solution to the underlying problem: that these villagers lacked access to the means needed for a better life. This case is not an outlier in India, nor is it in other middle-income countries such as Nigeria, China, Pakistan, and Indonesia. Those at the bottom of the pyramid are still too vulnerable, too fragile, and need more than just access to basic financial services.

Gender inequality is another form of inequality that impedes sustainable development. The International Monetary Fund (IMF) recently concluded that closing the wage gap between men and women would raise GDP by more than 10% in several countries. A recent report by the International Finance Corporation, the private sector arm of the World Bank, confirmed that better employment opportunities for women can contribute to increased profitability and productivity in the private sector. Overall, better jobs for women benefit individuals, families, communities, companies, and economies. With more income and financial independence, women can increase household spending on children's nutrition, health, and education.

Inequality has consequences in the long run. Recent research has shown that income inequality not only exacerbates societal inequalities, it also hinders a country's economic growth by making it difficult for lower-income households to invest in education and thereby lowering the nation's labour productivity. Some studies also argue that it has a dampening effect on total household consumption, as the rich spend a smaller percentage of their incomes than the poor. And in allowing the gap between the rich and the poor to widen, countries are putting the stability of their socioeconomic and political systems at risk in the long run. You do not need to look far to find situations in which economic inequality has undermined social, political, and economic stability.

Extreme inequality has sparked civil wars, mass migrations, and political revolutions before. Because of globalisation, more people than ever before are now aware that there are brighter economic prospects available in other countries. All over the world, economic migrants put their lives at great risk to find better opportunities in wealthier countries.

Growing inequality is a worldwide phenomenon – something that we are seeing in rich and poor countries alike. Clearly, this is another issue that has to be addressed. Not only must we work to reduce poverty further, we must also aim to realise inclusive growth. This is the next big challenge for the world.

... AND THE PLANET SUFFERS

As early as 1972, the world was given its first warning about the limits to our unrelenting pursuit of economic growth. A seminal report published by the Club of Rome, an international think tank consisting of leaders from a wide range of disciplines, outlined a doom scenario of disastrous resource shortages, gross economic inequalities, and eventual societal collapse if the world's exponential population growth and industrial consumption remained unchecked. The report, simply entitled *Limits to Growth*, was a wake-up call that sparked a lively public debate but nonetheless failed to gain broad traction at the international level.

In the 1980s, an increasing amount of evidence made it clear that human activities were having a serious impact on the environment and on climate change, especially through carbon dioxide emissions. Belief in the scientific evidence grew, and in 1992 the United Nations held its first conference on the environment and development in Rio de Janeiro, Brazil, which led to the signing of the United Nations Framework Convention on Climate Change, the first international environmental treaty ever negotiated. Since then, the UN has organised more than twenty of these conferences, the latest of which was held in Paris in 2015.

Climate change has a direct impact on poverty because the poor are the most vulnerable to the environment they live in. The world's poorest people depend most heavily and directly on primary natural resources (local forests, land, water, and the seas) and will suffer the most from adverse changes in their natural environment. Climate change has the potential to destroy their livelihoods by damaging the food and water systems that they rely on.

An issue that receives less attention worldwide is the loss of biodiversity. I have become more acquainted with this issue since chairing the board of the Dutch chapter of the International Union for Conservation of Nature. Biodiversity refers to the variety of life on earth: the genetic diversity in species and the diversity in ecosystems. It is important for us to protect our planet's biodiversity because it allows us to live healthy and happy lives by providing us with food, medicines, and a resilient environment. The rate at which human activity is destroying our planet's biodiversity is alarming. My own country, the Netherlands, offers a clear example: it has destroyed 85% of its biodiversity as a result of population pressure and agricultural practices over the centuries.

Poverty, inequality, and environmental degradation are closely interconnected: I am convinced that you cannot address these problems as separate issues or with separate institutional frameworks that presume a hierarchy of urgency. If you were to focus exclusively on eliminating poverty at the expense of protecting the environment, you would risk undermining the progress you have achieved as climate change intensifies and makes the poor even poorer. If we continue to pollute our seas and destroy marine biodiversity, millions of fishermen whose livelihood depends on the sea will be affected. The situation is no different for small farmers, who are vulnerable to the wild fluctuations in weather patterns that have emerged as a result of climate change.

There are organisations that focus exclusively on reducing poverty, which operate mainly in the international development world; there are also groups that focus only on protecting nature, which are part of the environmental movement; and then there are groups that place the highest priority on reducing inequality, traditionally dominant among NGOs; while groups that focus on economic growth are normally found in the private sector. This division of roles is a big mistake. It is my firm belief that you can only solve these worldwide problems with an integrated approach.

UNSUSTAINABLE TAXATION MODELS
AND PRACTICES

The tax rate in most developing countries is less than half of what it is in richer countries. Tax revenue in Europe, for example, accounts for 40% of GDP on average, while most developing countries have a tax-to-GDP ratio of only 20% or even lower. Taxes should be the single largest source of a nation's income, as it allows the government to provide its citizens with essential services. At the *Financing for Development* conference in Addis Ababa, it was agreed that developing economies would strengthen their tax collecting systems with the support of developed countries.

One problem in this area is the number of multinational companies that are not paying all of their taxes in the countries in which they operate, moving their profits instead to countries with minimal tax rates. I am not proud to say that the Netherlands is frequently used as a tax haven due to its numerous tax breaks and subsidies. This is a problem in particular for developing countries, which are deprived of a significant amount of money due to tax avoidance. Member countries of the Organisation for Economic Cooperation and Development (OECD) have committed themselves to delivering a tax framework to crack down on tax avoidance. If successful, this would be a nice example of putting all nations on an equal footing.

UNSUSTAINABLE BUSINESS MODELS
AND PRACTICES

With the breadth and urgency of the issues at hand, it is clear that re-evaluating and correcting the planet's course will require collaborative efforts on a variety of fronts. The private sector has an important role to play in this. Given the challenges we face, it is imperative that each business rethink its relationship to society. Maximising profits inevitably comes at the expense of humans or the environment – or both. The old notion of the earth as a bottomless well to fuel personal profit has been proven to be toxic and bankrupt. Our planet has ecological limits – limits that are currently being overstepped by human activity. While some businesses have been responding to the growing consumer shift towards sustainable practices, most of the solutions they have offered have been marginal and remain peripheral to their business. Instead, what needs to happen is for environmental and social standards to be integrated into the core of every business model and translated into concrete and measurable positive impacts. Companies will have to play an important role in helping to mobilise their peers in this changeover.

A PARADIGM SHIFT TOWARDS SUSTAINABLE DEVELOPMENT

2015 was a crucial year for sustainable development due to three important conferences that took place: the Financing for Development conference in Addis Ababa, the United Nations Sustainable Development Summit in New York, and the Climate Change Conference in Paris. Taken together, these three conferences represent a much-needed paradigm shift – a fundamental change in the way we approach the task of creating a better world.

A BRIEF HISTORY OF INTERNATIONAL ECONOMIC DEVELOPMENT

The first attempt to reach a global agreement on international economic development came in 1970. A study published earlier by Jan Tinbergen, the Dutch economist and Nobel prize winner, had concluded that the world would be able to eliminate poverty in thirty years if the richest countries in the world – mainly Europe, the US, Canada, and Japan – would transfer just one percent of their yearly national income to developing economies. Within the United Nations, it was agreed that governments of the developed world would aim to transfer a minimum of 0.7% of their GDP to developing economies. In practice, however, very few governments reached this target: as of 2015, only five countries had spent this minimum level on official development assistance (ODA). And even then, part of that 0.7% was used to finance the first-year costs of migrants in the receiving countries themselves, and another part was reserved for measures to address climate change. In general, the amount of ODA has barely grown over the last decade. In several countries – among others the Netherlands – there has even been a decrease.

Up to the turn of the millennium, the main question regarding development was "How much should we spend on poor people in developing economies?" But thereafter the focus shifted to measuring the outcomes of development aid. In 2000, the United Nations defined the Millennium Development Goals (MDGs): eight development objectives explicitly addressing extreme poverty and hunger, education, gender equality, child mortality, maternal health, major disease, environmental sustainability, and global development partnerships. Concrete sub-goals were introduced for each focus area, emphasising issues of human capital, infrastructure, and human rights in developing countries. These were clear objectives outlined in a language common to all parties, which gave an important incentive to focus on results. It was apparent that success would now be assessed on the basis of quantifiable results. Achieving the MDGs became the main focus of the developed world's ODA budgets.

THE SUSTAINABLE DEVELOPMENT GOALS

Fast forward to 2015, and we find ourselves in a new era. The global community has finally come around to the reality that it can no longer treat poverty and climate change as two unrelated challenges and that an integrated approach is the only way forward. After years of preparation and negotiation and against all odds, the member countries of the United Nations came together at the Sustainable Development Summit to define a direction for an integrated approach to solve world problems. It is an approach in which poverty reduction is inextricably linked to inclusiveness, climate change, and the environment. I believe this has triggered a real paradigm shift in the right direction. Today, countries are trying to define their national solutions on a global scale to address global problems.

If we are to collectively work towards creating a better world, we need concrete goals to strive for, landmarks that can help steer us on our way to the end goal. This is what the United Nations (UN) has provided when it presented the Sustainable Development Goals (SDGs) – also referred to as the Global Goals – to be achieved by 2030. The SDGs are 17 goals with 169 concrete sub-targets ranging from ending extreme poverty and eliminating gender gaps to promoting peaceful and inclusive societies. For example, SDG1 is to "end poverty in all its forms everywhere", which

Global Goals for Sustainable Development

1 NO POVERTY

2 ZERO HUNGER

3 GOOD HEALTH AND WELL-BEING

4 QUALITY EDUCATION

5 GENDER EQUALITY

6 CLEAN WATER AND SANITATION

7 AFFORDABLE AND CLEAN ENERGY

8 DECENT WORK AND ECONOMIC GROWTH

9 INDUSTRY, INNOVATION AND INFRASTRUCTURE

10 REDUCED INEQUALITIES

11 SUSTAINABLE CITIES AND COMMUNITIES

12 RESPONSIBLE CONSUMPTION AND PRODUCTION

13 CLIMATE ACTION

14 LIFE BELOW WATER

15 LIFE ON LAND

16 PEACE, JUSTICE AND STRONG INSTITUTIONS

17 PARTNERSHIPS FOR THE GOALS

include the sub-goal of ensuring equal access to economic opportunities as well as financial safety nets.

You can see the overlap between the SDGs and the points I have been covering so far. Though the sheer magnitude of its aims is perhaps intimidating, it is important to keep in mind that the SDGs are all interconnected, which means that success in one area will spill over into other areas. In addressing poverty (SDG1) – say with a job that provides a stable living wage that can feed, clothe, and educate a family – we can also attain the other goals related to hunger (SDG2), inequality (SDG10), health and well-being (SDG13), and education (SDG4), to name a few. Development strategies must focus on combinations of issues that are interdependent and thereby address the larger systems at work. In a later chapter I will demonstrate how development banks contribute to most of these goals.

The SDGs are especially remarkable in that the world now has global goals that acknowledge for the first time that all countries have problems deserving of attention and action. This has brought an end to the traditional North-South, West-East philanthropic model. Rich countries are no longer dictating to the poor; instead, all countries have a list of standards that they are being requested to meet. And while there are no sanctions if they fail to meet these standards, the UN member countries do have a transparent plan of attack with frequent updates on country progress. Countries will now pick their priorities and can be held accountable by their own citizens.

What is also clear is that developing governments need the private sector if they are going to achieve the Global Goals. The public sector approach to achieving global development objectives is now shifting from a simple ODA approach to a more effective strategy in which the public sector engages the private sector in order to complement each other as investors.

BREAKTHROUGH IN PARIS ON CLIMATE ACTION

Shortly after the terrible attacks in Paris that sadly left over one hundred innocent people dead, the United Nations Climate Change Conference (COP21) convened in December 2015. The fear at the time was that fewer people would attend – due to the threat of terrorism hanging over the city – and that emotions would negatively influence the outcome. However, under the excellent leadership of Christiana Figueres, the executive secretary of the UN Framework Convention on Climate Change, and through the skilled negotiating tactics of the French minister of foreign affairs, Laurent Fabius, the outcome was better than anyone had ever expected.

In Paris, 185 countries managed to reach a historic agreement to limit global warming to a maximum of two degrees Celsius (with a strong preference for keeping it below 1.5 degrees). As with the SDGs, each country will be expected to present and execute its own plan, including how the plan will be financed. The progress made on these plans will be evaluated every five years. The UN's Green Climate Fund will raise funds from developed countries' governments that will rise to US $91 billion each year by 2020 to help developing countries make the changes needed to adapt to the climate goals.

The final climate agreement also explicitly recognises the role that forests play in offsetting human activity. This was a clear call to action for countries to preserve standing forests. In the last two decades, various studies have estimated that changes in land usage, including deforestation and forest degradation, have accounted for 12-20% of global greenhouse gas emissions. Clearly, this was an area that needed to be addressed. The COP21 agreement provides for public and private funding for tropical and subtropical countries if they succeed in reducing their emissions from deforestation and forest degradation. The explicit inclusion of this mechanism, known as REDD+, builds on years of work by governments, indigenous peoples, civil society, and funding institutions to find ways to positively incentivise countries to reduce carbon emissions and conserve their standing forests at the same time.

Almost everyone involved in the climate change discussion agrees that the single most effective measure to bring down carbon dioxide emissions would be to put a price on it. If the price were set above US $50 per ton, the impact on consumers and producers would be immediate. Regrettably, the countries at the climate conference failed to come to an agreement on implementing such a tax or price. This may not be a realistic worldwide goal today, but the fact that different parts of the world – including Australia, California, and certain regions in China – are beginning to experiment with setting prices or taxes on carbon gives me great hope.

FINANCING DEVELOPMENT THROUGH BLENDED FINANCE

One month before the UN Sustainable Development Summit, the third international Financing for Development conference was held in Addis Ababa, Ethiopia, to draw attention to the crucial role of the private sector. Given that ODA funds are growing scarcer and that such funds are also being used to pay for the intake of immigrants and refugees, it is clear that developing governments must have access to the means and the resources of the private sector if they are going to achieve the SDGs. The question is finally being approached on equal terms, with both the rich and the poor, the public and the private being held accountable for their roles in addressing development challenges.

The Addis Ababa conference was the first time I heard the private sector mentioned as a prominent driving force for development. That is a real breakthrough, as in all my forty years of working in international development, I had always witnessed a deep suspicion against the private sector. The belief that institutions with profit targets are not capable of doing anything beneficial for society had remained entrenched for a long time. But at this conference, I saw and sensed that governments were now beginning to recognise the potential capacity of the private sector to contribute to societal well-being.

Circumstances help, of course. Over the last 25 years, donor countries' ODA as a percentage of total capital flows into emerging markets has decreased from more than 50% to less than 10% as private capital flows have become more and more important. It is not that ODA flows have declined – indeed, they have remained quite stable in absolute terms – but all other flows have increased significantly. So governments in developed countries are becoming aware that in order to make the most of their ODA, they must focus on enabling private sector investment in developing economies. If governments of developing economies can build a robust environment for entrepreneurial endeavours, development banks can help finance this transition.

The combination of public and private finance, referred to as "blended finance", was the focus of the discussions in Addis Ababa. The public financing comes from received ODA or in many cases takes the form of explicit subsidies. With government or philanthropic help, development projects that may have otherwise been "unbankable" – in other words, too risky for an investment – can now be financed. The key is to blend government money with private sector money in order to catalyse as much capital as possible from private sources. When these projects mature, development banks such as FMO step in and work towards the Global Goals. In FMO's case, we try to directly impact the goals related to energy, food security, and economic growth, which in turn affects poverty, climate, and inequality.

International conferences such as the one in Addis Ababa are increasingly bringing companies and local governments together as cooperative strategisers. In doing so, they are ensuring that the private sector takes its share of the responsibility of attaining the SDGs.

Admittedly, I was initially sceptical about the frenzy of conferences being planned for 2015. Could we really bring together tens of thousands of people and effectively discuss the problems of climate change, sustainability, and economic inequality? Just think of the carbon footprint generated from gathering all these people from all over the world!* Yet each conference proved to be a valuable investment with a promising step in the right direction. From the GDP agreement of the 1970s to the MDGs, we have made progress, and now each of these conferences has delivered explicit agreements and objectives. They have provided the groundwork, and we stand crouched in anticipation. Some problems are still far from being solved, but what is stopping us from making an even more impressive leap forward? The Global Goals themselves have 169 targets – an intimidating prospect. But rather than fixate on the overwhelming mountain of problems the world faces, we must consider

---

* FMO offsets 100% of its own ecological footprint – including air and car travel and the energy used in our offices – and we contribute to carbon reduction by investing in reforestation and renewable energy.

the interconnectedness of these issues and acknowledge the urgency to act lest we seriously damage our chance of a sustainable and equitable future. In addition to offering a fantastic investment opportunity, financing a better world requires the proactive involvement of development banks to reach the Global Goals in time.

ACCELERATING THE SHIFT TO SUSTAINABLE DEVELOPMENT

When governments, civil society, businesses, and banks each define how they aim to contribute to a better world, they will collectively have the mass needed to realise the global vision of a world where nine billion people can thrive within the limitations of our planet.

THE ROLE OF BUSINESSES

More than ever before, consumers are turning to the green or sustainable option. A growing number of people want the products they buy to be produced fairly by companies that mirror their concern for the future. Even in finance, consumers are taking an increasingly active role in investment decisions, insisting that their money be invested in projects that generate a positive impact on society. Though some businesses have made changes to meet their clients' needs, few have integrated their environmental and social contributions into the core of their business model. From a business perspective, this is pure folly. The growing consumer momentum is not some fleeting trend – it is the future. And those companies that do not jump on the bandwagon will be left behind.

I am optimistic about this movement. Some large multinationals have chosen this path – most notably Unilever. Unilever CEO Paul Polman has dedicated enormous amounts of his time to contribute to the discussion on a sustainable world, making it clear that Unilever is fully engaged in the shift to sustainability. Unilever was an inspiration for me when FMO was defining its ambitious goals. The company has set its sights on doubling its sales while halving its carbon footprint. This is a bold statement for a multinational whose products are bought by two billion people yearly. The impact of this is huge, whether in palm oil or in agriculture at large. The top ten companies in the Dow Jones sustainability index include Unilever, and I am proud to say that Dutch multinationals are over-represented in this index.

The next step that companies need to take is to incorporate the value of natural capital into their balance sheets. This will enable a clear and undeniable relationship to be established between business and the natural environment, making it crystal clear why it is in the interests of the private sector to integrate sustainable standards into businesses' core strategies. Just such a new approach to natural capital is being developed by a worldwide coalition of finance, business, accounting, academia, and civil society known as the Natural Capital Coalition, which I currently chair. In July 2016, the NCC presented its natural capital protocol that can be used by businesses. Once companies understand the role of the environment in their core processes and the value of that relationship on their balance sheets, financiers will be able to use that information in assessing their investments. This will take sustainability to a new level and make it part of the core business of a company and a real impetus for sustainable development. In the end, it is critical for companies to ensure that their net impact on the environment is positive throughout their entire value chain.

THE ROLE OF GOVERNMENTS

Governments are essential in supporting and pushing business towards sustainability. How can governments influence decision-making in this area? To start with, tax can be a powerful instrument for influencing business decisions. As I mentioned before, a sufficiently high carbon tax could make a real difference. As the methodologies develop, similar schemes could be applied to other natural resources using, natural capital accounting to monitor exactly how companies consume resources in their business processes. Subsidies to encourage good behaviour can be helpful as well. Government measures do, however, raise the question: how long will they remain in effect? Until now, governments have been erratic in the way they have subsidised renewable energy.

Governments can also influence businesses by setting policies, standards, and minimum requirements on the products they sell or on the social and environmental effects they produce. Another way governments can shape business incentives is by controlling what they buy from businesses and by requiring certain social and environmental standards to be met before they acquire goods and services. Policies focused on innovation can also help to stimulate the market.

In the case of emerging markets and developing economies, having a solid legal framework and independent arbitrage are indispensable for attracting business investment. Governments should demand transparency in annual reports and require frameworks such as integrated reporting, which would be an important step in the right direction. The best-case scenario would have the government set a national goal of having a net-zero ecological footprint throughout the entire value chain of all products consumed in the country. The Dutch government could, for example, have a policy in place to offset the footprint of a small Peruvian farmer providing cacao for the chocolate consumed in the Netherlands.

THE ROLE OF CIVIL SOCIETY

The Consumer Perspective

Consumers can be a powerful force for change. Businesses fear consumer boycotts, and today, reputation is more important than ever. If consumers were to collectively vote with their feet and only buy fair-trade products, for example, this would transform the market and thereby also completely change business practices. We are already seeing the demand for fair trade products and sustainable food growing faster than the market average in many countries. The shift in consumer behaviour is, however, a frustratingly slow process and one that isn't always easy to predict. In the end, the cost of externalities should be included in the products that consumers buy. Likewise, consumers should be held responsible for their own ecological footprint and aim to bring it down to zero.

The NGO Perspective

NGOs come in many different shapes and flavours. I distinguish four main types.

The first are NGOs that function as think tanks and produce fact-based (scientific) reports, recommendations, and visions such as the World

Business Council for Sustainable Development, the Rocky Mountain Institute, the World Resource Institute, and the International Union for Conservation of Nature. These organisations are great sources of knowledge that can improve our insight into sustainable development priorities as well as ways to reach the Global Goals.

Then there are the NGOs that execute projects on the ground in developing countries such as Care International, Root Capital and BRAC Bangladesh. These NGOs generally focus on working with local communities and operate at the base of the economic pyramid. Some of these NGOs work closely with companies, helping them reach out to low-income producers and/or communities.

Other NGOs such as the Global Reporting Initiative, the Natural Capital Coalition, and the International Integrated Reporting Council develop guidelines for reporting, tools for decision-making, and certification for products. Their work is instrumental in creating internationally accepted standards.

And finally there are the NGOs with political agendas. These organisations lobby for various causes, using local and sometimes worldwide campaigns. Examples include Oxfam, Greenpeace, Friends of the Earth, and Global Witness. These organisations fulfill an international advocacy role for various populations and issues worldwide, mobilising citizens and serving as whistle-blowers.

Until several years ago, the relationship between development banks and NGOs – in particular the political ones – had been one of distant colleagues working in similar fields. Recently, however, those NGOs have begun to hold development banks such as FMO accountable for upholding its environmental, social, and governance standards. Development finance institutions have much to learn about how to work with NGOs, and I am confident that this relationship will mature with time as transparency on both sides improves.

FINANCING SUSTAINABLE DEVELOPMENT

We are now approaching the core of this book: how do you finance sustainable development? As the backbone of the economic system, financial institutions provide the financial services and credit needed to empower entrepreneurs and their businesses with the tools and resources to grow. Financial institutions can be change agents and accelerate shifts in society, adapting their own processes but also inspiring their customers and competitors to take action. Without the active involvement of financial institutions, we as a society run the risk of missing the boat on creating a more sustainable future.

Bridging Governments, the Financial Sector, and the Private Sector

The public and private sectors have widely diverging ideas about important issues, and it often seems as though they speak completely different languages. The private sector approaches things from the bottom up: where is the demand and how can it best be fulfilled? The public sector thinks top down: what do I see as a (politically) relevant problem and how can I intervene to solve that problem? At the risk of making a sweeping statement, governments mistrust profits and businesses detest market interventions.

This is why development finance institutions (DFIs) are needed to help bridge the divide. Since their very inception, DFIs have been serving as the link between the private sector and governments. FMO has been doing so for forty years. DFIs have both the competencies and the mandate to play this role.

In the coming years, DFI activity will surpass governments' ODA programmes in terms of the size of capital flows. This makes it all the more urgent for us to clearly define a division of roles between the two worlds. Governments should increasingly take on the role of enablers for the private sector and where necessary mitigate the highest risks, while DFIs should focus on investing in businesses as well as on mobilising funds from institutional investors for sustainable development.

CONCLUSION

In this chapter I have explained the profound change that has occurred in the way we think about international development aid, climate change, and biodiversity. The Global Goals can only be met when all actors take their responsibility and are held accountable. Development finance institutions have a crucial role to play in bridging the gap between the main actors involved. Blended finance can play an important role in this, as I will explain in chapter five.

SUSTAINABLE DEVELOPMENT AS A BUSINESS OPPORTUNITY

In chapter two, I described the breakthrough in the international negotiations surrounding the Global Goals. I am convinced that the need for businesses to contribute to this better world is not only clear and urgent but unavoidable. "Business as usual" is no longer acceptable.

What I now want to draw attention to are the huge opportunities that sustainable development offers businesses. Drawing on FMO's experience as well as my personal involvement, I will describe what I believe is needed for companies to integrate societal and environmental sustainability into the core of their business. I conclude the chapter with the challenges that businesses face in emerging markets and developing economies. Although these markets offer exciting opportunities, they often lack well-functioning judicial and institutional frameworks that can safeguard social and environmental standards and human rights.

THE US $1.5 TRILLION OPPORTUNITY

Laying the framework for a society that responsibly lives within the confines of our planet is going to require a huge amount of investment. According to accepted estimates, the amount of existing investment flows and additional investments needed to refocus on sustainable production and inclusive finance is 1-2% of global GDP, and the amount of investments needed in countries with a per capita income of less than US $12 per day is around US $1.5 trillion. About two-thirds of these investments should go to infrastructure, clean energy, telecommunications, roads, and ports, and the final one-third will be needed for areas such as healthcare, education, food security, drinking water, sanitation, and the protection and restoration of ecosystems.

The figures being bandied about, which are in the order of trillions of dollars, are both mind-boggling and worrisome. While these are general estimates that are bound to fluctuate, what these numbers do make clear is the magnitude of the investment shortage at hand.

Rather than seeing this as a gap, however, I feel that businesses should look at the situation as an opportunity. If existing businesses do not adapt, new ones will move in to help facilitate the changes necessary to make our societies sustainable. Whether we are talking about the way people live, the way they connect, or the way they learn or move around, the fundamental factor to remember is that one size does not fit all. Each region has its own set of development needs. These intricacies and nuances open up opportunities for different businesses within each sector, each country, and each city. Financing will be necessary to enable businesses to seize these opportunities, but businesses will be the ones to carry it out.

Encouragingly, some important businesses and financial institutions are shifting from a reactive to a proactive role, selecting projects and formulating solutions that address the complex and deeply intertwined nature of poverty, economic growth, and environmental degradation. However, at present, this movement has not gained nearly enough traction. Below, I outline the concrete steps that businesses must take to shift to a sustainable business approach.

THE STEPS NEEDED TO CREATE A SUSTAINABLE BUSINESS

If increasing shareholder value is your only goal, life is pretty straightforward: you limit your decisions to maximising that single target. Doing so will allow your business to thrive, but at what cost? At the expense of other people? The environment? The future?

Integrate the Global Goals into Your Mission

Businesses need to ask themselves the following question: how do we need to change in order to address societal needs, and what is needed to finance them? It is important for businesses to start by building up their knowledge base on sustainable development, entering into new networks, and gaining experience. Based on these new insights, companies must then make sustainable development an integral part of their mission. In concrete terms, this means determining how they intend to contribute to the Global Goals and incorporating them into their business plans and budgets. Setting the boundaries and scope for this exercise is crucial. In order to maximise their impact, companies should also consider their full value chain in their plans.

In the long run, the new business opportunities created by this new way of doing business will also contribute to shareholder value. Some companies have started this journey with exclusion lists, as FMO has done in the past, excluding investments in certain areas of business ranging from weapons to unsustainable fisheries. Only by taking the next step and embedding sustainability in the core of your business will it be possible for profit making to synthesise with contributing to a better world.

Make Profit

Why should businesses make a profit? Is it really necessary? And how much profit is enough? Profit is a precondition for businesses to attract investors, as investors require compensation for the risk of not getting their money back and for the inconvenience of having to delay their consumption. In order to build a sustainable business, therefore, profit is key.

In theory, a company could define a minimum level of profits that could be used to compensate its investors and at the same time aim to maximise its impact on society and on the environment. This was the starting point of FMO's discussions with the Dutch Ministry of Finance, our main shareholder, on the level of profits we should target. We agreed on an average five-year return of slightly more than 6%. It is no coincidence that several other development finance institutions also target a financial return of about 6%.

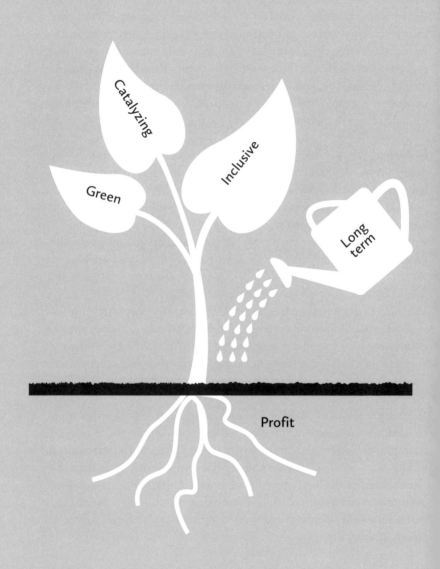

Catalyzing

Green

Inclusive

Long term

Profit

Profit is important because it allows companies to grow autonomously – i.e., without charity or government subsidies. Growth enables companies to reach economies of scale in their operations. For a development bank, the ability to finance sustainable development entrepreneurship on a growing scale allows it to generate social and environmental impact on a growing scale.

In addition, a profit objective requires financial discipline. When a company is loss-making, it either takes too much risk or incurs costs that are too high, or both. The amount of capital steadily dwindles, with the result that in the medium term, the company shrinks in size or disappears altogether, thereby generating no impact whatsoever on the society or the environment.

To attract sustainable investors, companies need to demonstrate that profits can be combined with the aim of having a positive social and environmental impact. Nobody is willing to invest in a loss-making model. It is important to demonstrate that profit and impact can be combined so that others will be persuaded to follow the impact model. Over the years, evaluations conducted by development banks have shown that the vast majority of companies that realise their return expectations also realise their impact expectations.

Measure Your Impact

When the core of your business is generating societal impact, it is crucial to make your aims explicit. How do you define impact? In terms of the environment, quantitative targets can be set to reduce carbon dioxide emissions and manage water usage, land use and waste handling. With regard to societal impact, I believe that creating fair jobs is one of the most important ways that companies can make a difference. Jobs can lift people out of poverty and give their lives meaning – that is the case the world over. A steady income allows a person to focus on more than just their next meal; they can pay for healthcare and education for themselves and/or for their children. From a firm financial base, they have the potential to build upwards. Why else would politicians around the world say that creating jobs is their highest priority?

As an organisation, FMO sets quantitative targets for generating jobs and for reducing or avoiding carbon dioxide emissions. These quantitative targets go further than simply monitoring and reporting on these indicators: they are concrete objectives that make it easier for us to steer our clients in the right direction and to clearly communicate our aims to our stakeholders. This is not without its potential pitfalls, and it is important to always consider how effective a metric is for your goal. When job creation is blindly followed, for example, a company that needs to reduce headcount in order to become more efficient would lose its eligibility for receiving finance. Quantitative targets also risk becoming a scorecard of sorts, as has happened before at FMO when measuring our development impact. Like any game, people learned to play it well, leading to situations in which we saw great improvements in the score on paper without the same impact in reality.

Since 2015, FMO has adopted and implemented internationally accepted guidelines for integrated reporting to explain how the bank creates value. Integrated reporting goes significantly further than the traditional financial reporting required of companies, as it obliges companies to show how they implement their strategy and make decisions to remain on track to meet their targets. FMO has chosen to report in this way because our stakeholders are very interested in our non-financial results and the way we manage our business. Integrated reporting is still quite new in the area of development. I am convinced that development banks should be frontrunners in this area because they need to be as transparent as possible on who they do business with as well as how they achieve their results. If development banks establish themselves as models of transparency, businesses and governments are more likely to follow suit.

Operationalise Sustainable Development Standards

If a company aims to generate a lasting impact in the area of sustainable development, it must uphold certain environmental, social, and governance standards – commonly referred to as ESG standards – and encourage or insist that its suppliers do the same. ESG management begins with a focus on risk and over time evolves into recognising opportunities. When a company clearly defines it relationship and responsibility to society, being successful depends on ESG standards becoming part of the core of your business. Development banks are in just such a process, and other companies can benefit from their experience.

The first big challenge is involving everyone in your organisation in the transition to a truly sustainable entity. It took us some time at FMO to realise how important it was to not just talk the talk but also walk the walk. Until then, we had asked something of our clients that we did not always fully understand ourselves. Although FMO had introduced environmental, social, and governance standards earlier, not everyone had been convinced as to why they were necessary and how it would benefit their work. But we realised that if we wanted to bring about a change in our clients, we would first have to change ourselves. The vision would have to be clear, the approach consistent, and the commitment complete – for the entire organisation. The implementation would only work if we put environmental and social sustainability at the core of our strategy and our business. The same holds true for companies in relation to the businesses in their supply chain: in order to persuade their suppliers of the need for sustainable development, the companies themselves must set the example.

Create Fair Jobs

Companies are the foundation of economic growth and job creation: 90% of the jobs created are in the private sector. Of course, simply creating jobs is not enough. Companies must ensure that working conditions are acceptable in terms of health and safety standards, and the jobs should be reasonably paid. There is an important distinction to be made between a 'minimum wage' and a 'living wage'. Whereas a minimum wage is a rate that can be set arbitrarily, a living wage takes into account what someone needs to pay for his or her basic needs. In many countries, there is a discrepancy between the two, with the lower minimum wage being favoured. From a moral point of view, companies should pay a living wage. It is also the responsibility of companies to check the working conditions at companies in their value chain. This is something that we are seeing more and more businesses starting to do.

Create Positive Impact on the Environment

Companies will need to take into account how their activities impact the environment both in their investment decisions and in their daily operations. A good start would be to reduce the amount of greenhouse gases they emit and to optimise the use of their resources. When companies start to focus on these themes, they often discover that reducing energy and resource use leads to a more efficient process in which they actually save costs. I think this is a great example of how a positive impact goes hand in hand with positive financial return. We can take the process a step further by moving to a 'circular economy' as well as a 'cradle-to-cradle' approach that allows resources to be reused as much as possible and that transforms waste into fuel. This approach should result in a positive impact on the environment.

Increase Inclusiveness

For many companies, it is not readily apparent how incorporating inclusiveness into their strategy will benefit not just the entire society but also their business. By increasing the diversity of their workforce in terms of gender, nationality, and age in all layers of their organisation, companies have access to a variety of viewpoints and a diverse set of skills and experience. Moreover, by mirroring the society they live in, employees can more easily identify with potential customers and thereby assess their needs and demands. This is why it is advantageous for companies to identify and change the implicit processes and procedures entrenched in their organisation that impede certain groups.

Thinking about inclusiveness from a broader societal perspective, businesses must work together with their stakeholders to identify excluded populations and actively develop or identify business models geared towards reaching out to them. One way this can be done is to look at how a company's products and services can serve people living below the poverty line. Businesses can simplify their products for those at the base of the pyramid (e.g. cheap and simple mobile phones) or even introduce smaller packaging to make their products more affordable, although buying in bulk remains cheaper. New and innovative payment methods are another way to give low-income households access to products that are beyond their reach. Successful models have recently emerged that use mobile payment systems in which the customer's use of the product is limited to instalments, similar to prepaid phone plans. This is essentially a hitherto unexploited market opportunity for businesses – another example of how sustainable development can benefit all those involved.

One of the major obstacles poor people face are high transaction costs. Because their transactions tend to be smaller in size and often require more complex information gathering, lower-income households generally pay much higher costs per transaction than richer people. This is certainly the case for financial products, where the costs per transaction are fixed (e.g. the cost of a transaction of US $100 is the same as the cost of a US $5,000 transaction). In addition, information on the creditworthiness of poor people – such as their character, assets, sales, etc. – is costly to gather. Devising innovative solutions for excluded groups should be part of good business practice. One thing is clear: new technology will be crucial. A good example of how technology has transformed the economic reality of poor people is the Mpesa project in Kenya. Mpesa is a mobile platform for money transfers that is digitalised, which has not only reduced the cost of money transfers by 90% in many cases but also made such transfers more secure. These are the kinds of solutions that are needed in areas such as electricity, water, education, and health provision.

Pay Appropriate Taxes

Government tax income relies heavily on the fundamental contributions of businesses as they pay tax on things such as value added and profits. Governments then use this tax income to invest in education, healthcare, and infrastructure to improve the lives of their citizens. Whether governments make use of tax revenue in an optimal way should be of no concern to businesses or banks, which have a responsibility as members of society to pay their fair share of public services that ultimately benefit them as well. Ensuring that companies pay appropriate taxes is an important part of financing sustainable development.

DOING BUSINESS IN EMERGING MARKETS AND DEVELOPING ECONOMIES

Accelerating sustainable development in emerging markets and developing economies is crucial to achieving the Global Goals because 90% of the growth in the world population and global GDP is expected to take place there in the coming years. The continuing growth of the middle class in these countries will have a huge impact on consumption patterns. Middle-class households generally consume more meat* and more energy (through products such as cars and electric devices), which makes it crucial for green investments to play a larger role there. At the same time, the overwhelming majority of the world's poor live in developing economies. To reach the Global Goals in time, therefore, both the major challenges and the major economic opportunities lie in emerging markets and developing economies.

Weak Institutional Frameworks

What makes it challenging to work in emerging markets and developing economies is the lack of fully functioning government institutions. More often than not, what remains less developed in lower-income countries is their institutional framework – the system of formal laws, informal conventions, customs, and norms that shape socio-economic activity and behaviour. In general, their legal institutions lack potency and independence, and the social security system is inadequate. Pension funds are still a nascent industry in such countries, and capital markets are often insignificant if not altogether non-existent. The absence of energy and transportation infrastructure also makes it difficult to conduct business, and education and skill levels are relatively low. However, there is good news: most countries appear to be on a steady positive trajectory. The World Bank has shown that in most countries there have been positive improvements in access to finance and energy as well in government regulations that influence the business climate.

Due to the dearth of robust legal systems and the lack of effective regulation on environmental and social issues in these countries, foreign businesses can take advantage of these lower standards and requirements. To push international businesses to operate responsibly, a number of NGOs and international organisations have been developing various standards and guidelines that together make up a comprehensive framework. The OECD guidelines on responsible business were developed for multinational companies and other businesses involved in foreign investment, providing recommendations on how businesses should deal with issues such as human rights, employment, the environment, corruption, and competition. Another important set of

---

* The meat industry happens to emit the highest amount of carbon dioxide emissions of all industries.

guidelines are the IFC Performance Standards which focus more on the larger investors in projects and include guidelines on dealing with land rights and indigenous communities. Further, there are standards established by the International Labor Organization and the United Nations as well as guidelines developed by sectors and industries themselves such as the Equator Principles (produced for and by the financial industry), the Principles of Responsible Investment (produced for and by institutional investors), and guidelines for the soy and palm oil industries. All these standards are regularly refined and updated, which requires businesses to remain informed and to constantly adapt. Although the business climate in poorer countries is not optimal, good and sustainable business can be done. Development banks have financed thousands of companies operating in emerging markets and developing economies that have proven to be models in adhering to international standards.

Limited Scope of Influence

For the private sector, the ability to influence societal good in a country is in theory limited to the scope of each project or each business itself and to the direct and indirect impacts and factors within each environment. To believe that the same can be achieved at the same rate in different countries is a gross oversimplification and does little justice to the complexities and intricacies that lie within each country's present and historical conditions. When operating in different countries – each with their own political system and their own culture – it is difficult to know where to draw the line between guidance and interference.

FMO selects projects that aim to facilitate change so that they can provide an inspirational and replicable example for their peers. While FMO cannot change a particular country's tax system, for example, we do check whether the companies we finance pay appropriate taxes. FMO frequently invests in – or with – entrepreneurs who are among the richest in the country. We cannot change the fact that a financial oligarchy of families exists in a particular country, but we conduct a thorough check on all our clients to see if they are directly involved in politics. FMO does its utmost to avoid connections with corruption: we do an in-depth integrity check on all our clients and their relations. At the end of the day, FMO focuses on the benefits that these projects bring to the country because we believe that they add value to the which in turn accelerates social and environmental change. In doing so, FMO not only runs financial risks, we also run the risk that, despite our scrutiny, our clients are involved in one way or another with corruption or other practices that run counter to the standards we apply. The only way to avoid these risks is to avoid financing risky projects altogether. The only thing that a development bank can do is try everything within its power to mitigate these risks as much as possible.

Handling Human Rights

One of the highest priorities that businesses should set for themselves is respecting human rights, because their social license to operate depends on doing so. In the due diligence process completed before financing a project, a development bank will always pay attention to human rights such as the prohibition of child labour, the elimination of discrimination, and the right of all workers to health, safety and security. Development banks apply the UN Guiding Principles on Business and Human Rights which distinguish the government's duty to protect the human rights of its citizens from the responsibility of businesses to respect human rights in all its activities and to aid victims of corporate abuse. Applying these principles is an essential step in making any project sustainable.

Given the huge number of infrastructure developments that are needed to reach the Global Goals, the support of local communities and their free, prior, and informed consent (FPIC) are crucial to their implementation. The transition to renewable energy also introduces an additional complexity. While in the past, most energy resources such as coal, oil, and gas were drawn from the earth's crust, today's renewable energy sources such as hydro, wind, and solar power rely on infrastructure that is above the ground. Communities are increasingly confronted with the question of whether they want to allow such projects in their vicinity.

This is not unique to developing economies. All over the world, protests are taking place against the visual pollution that wind, solar, and hydro energy projects cause. Governments should be playing an important role in balancing national and local interests in this issue. In democratic countries with sound legal systems, the possibility of arbitration and a reasonably fair process can be expected, but in countries that lack strong judicial institutions and legislation, it often becomes difficult for the local parties involved to solve these issues in a fair and peaceful way.

Facing an NGO Campaign

FMO recently found itself targeted by a large-scale NGO campaign against an energy project in Honduras that we were funding. It was the first time in the bank's 46-year history that anything of the sort had happened. The campaigners demanded that the financiers of the Agua Zarca energy project – FMO, Finnfund, and the Central American Bank for Economic Integration (CABEI)—pull out their investments immediately.

The campaign gained widespread publicity when a key leader of the protests against the Agua Zarca project, Berta Cáceres, was murdered on 3 March 2016. Cáceres had been the coordinator and co-founder of the Council of Indigenous Peoples of Honduras (COPINH) and a well-respected human rights activist and environmentalist. The NGOs linked the murder directly to her role in the protests against the project, which was picked up by the local and international media. The Agua Zarca project was depicted as the largest hydro dam in Central America, and it was alleged that the dam would flood large areas of land owned by the local Lenca population. The campaigners claimed that the indigenous people had not been consulted prior to the project. These accusations were especially painful for us because Agua Zarca was actually a small, run-of-the-river hydro project that had been redesigned based on extensive discussions with the local communities. No land was to be flooded.Based on the carefully executed process of consultation, the financiers including FMO had concluded that the majority of the affected population were in favour of the project.

Three days after Cáceres' murder, the first demonstrators appeared on FMO's front steps. Waving posters in the air, they shouted 'FMO murderers!'. This was difficult for me to watch because we are a bank that works earnestly to improve people's lives. The people who work for FMO believe passionately in creating a better world and a better future for all. Our projects are meant to unite communities, not divide them. We had never faced anything like this before. As the situation in Honduras deteriorated further, however, we eventually decided to end our involvement in Agua Zarca.

Free, Prior, and Informed Consent

One of the key arguments used by the NGOs in their campaign against the Agua Zarca project was that it had not followed the Free, Prior and Informed Consent (FPIC) procedure. This same argument is often used with other infrastructure projects when land rights and/or indigenous communities are involved.

FPIC is based on the principle that an indigenous community has the right to give or withhold its consent to proposed projects that may affect the land they traditionally own, occupy, or otherwise use. The IFC Performance Standards provide practical guidance for private sector actors on how to apply an FPIC procedure prior to the start of a project. Many NGO stakeholders do not accept the developer's FPIC processes and are of the opinion that FPIC should be obtained by the government rather than by the developer *before* offering the concession to the developer. Even if an FPIC procedure is used, however, there is no guarantee that conflicts will not arise before, during, or after the implementation of a project.

A number of issues surrounding FPIC are not clearly defined. When exactly is FPIC required? What is the definition of 'indigenous'? What if a small minority are the only ones against a project? How does one define a majority? Who represents the indigenous communities? This remains a grey area and one that is complicated to define because there are no arbitrage processes and no mediation institutions to turn to for help in answering these questions. When conflicts surrounding projects do arise, the disagreement usually pertains to these issues.

There are a few countries in the world that have integrated FPIC into the local law – including Peru, Australia, and the Philippines. This does mean that the overwhelming majority of countries do not apply the FPIC procedure before granting licences for infrastructure projects in indigenous areas. In these situations, the project owner and the financiers must fill this void together.

There is no doubt that the responsibility for solving issues between landowners and communities in an acceptable manner lies with the government. That would indeed be the ideal solution.

In reality, however, this would entail that far too many projects are simply not implemented, making it impossible to foster sustainable development and reach the Global Goals. By ruling out the majority of projects, you obstruct the main avenues of job creation, clean energy production, and so on.

A project's due diligence is completed before construction begins. The implementation of a project itself changes the local dynamics and power relations, as it introduces the question of who will get the jobs; who will benefit from the schools, clinics, and access to energy; and – sometimes – who will receive compensation for relocation or damages. Unfortunately, what we see in practice is that projects sometimes attract people who see an opportunity to receive compensation for damages they did not suffer.

NGOs tend to focus on indigenous and local community land rights because these are the rights that often come under pressure from large projects, especially in the cases of renewable energy, infrastructure, and agriculture, as they can require vast stretches of land. The seizure of land by a nation, state, or organisation, especially when done illegally or unfairly, is popularly called 'land grabbing'. NGOs play a crucial role here in preventing this injustice because local (indigenous) communities often need the help of organised support to defend their rights. At the same time, when NGOs focus on the rights of the underrepresented, it could lead them to lose sight of the balance that needs to be struck between the interests of small minorities and the interests of the large majority. Both the private sector and NGOs must take steps to improve this dialogue if they are to come up with better solutions. The consultation process needs to change in the future for the benefit of all people involved – both the minority and the majority. Increased transparency on both sides is key to engaging in a constructive dialogue. For the developer and DFIs, this means being more transparent at an earlier stage about the impact of the projects and the implementation of international standards. For the NGOs, this means being more transparent in the way they select their partners, who their partners represent, and what codes of conduct are agreed upon.

For FMO, the world after the Agua Zarca case is a very different one indeed. We must become better at reaching out to NGOs in a constructive way and also at improving the way we explain why and how we execute our projects and achieve our impact objectives. I believe that this issue of facilitating a constructive dialogue requires work on both sides. We should in any case not let this distract us from achieving our common goal of a better world.

CONCLUSION

It is very clear to me that in order to reach the Global Goals by 2030, the nature of business has to change fundamentally – and fast. The good news is that many businesses, multinationals, and SMEs are making that change as we speak. But we still have a long road to travel. The required changes that I described in this chapter – incorporating the Global Goals into business strategies, creating and monitoring fair jobs, being aware of one's environmental impact, becoming more inclusive – are all achievable and conceivably profitable. As said, emerging markets and developing economies are crucial because it is there that the bulk of the world's economic growth will take place. They are also the countries where innovation is much needed and where inclusiveness is crucial if we are to stem the increase in inequality. As these are also the countries where simply upholding local regulations is not always enough, international standards must be applied in order to create a positive impact in those markets.

FINANCING SUSTAINABLE DEVELOPMENT

Up to this point, I have examined how and why businesses should become sustainable. It is now time to turn our attention towards the role of the financial sector in enabling sustainable development. The work that will be generated by efforts to meet the Climate Goals and the Global Goals will require financing. While governments should play an important role, the bulk of the financing will have to come from financial institutions such as banks (including development banks), insurance companies, pension funds, and impact investors. The crucial issue I want to consider in this chapter is how the financial sector can contribute to financing sustainable development.

THE ROLE OF THE FINANCIAL SECTOR

In chapter three, I mentioned the huge amount of investment needed to meet both the Global Goals and the Climate Goals in time. This is also a tremendous opportunity for financiers. The main sources of financing will be governments, businesses, and household savings. The latter is managed by the financial sector in the form of bank accounts, life insurance policies, pension funds, and so on.

At the end of the day, these bank accounts, pension policies, etc. are *our* savings, which means that *we* have the right to determine what happens with our money. As savers, we therefore have the ability to influence how our money impacts the world. There are those who actively partake in 'impact investing', which refers to investing with the aim of creating a positive impact on social or environmental issues. I will return to this topic towards the end of this chapter.

Usually, governments are responsible for investing in healthcare, education, drinking water, sanitation, and transportation infrastructure as well as food security and ecosystems. Once the business cases in these areas become profitable, the private sector can step in. Governments are mainly financed through taxes – an area that is in dire need of improvement, as mentioned above. The solution to the problem of tax avoidance must come from both sides: governments must develop more effective tax collection mechanisms and raise taxes to generate more income, and businesses must shoulder their tax responsibilities and stop exploiting tax loopholes. Experts have estimated that implementing certain measures would lead to a doubling of government tax income in developing economies.

Looking at what is necessary in achieving the Global Goals, we can make a distinction between social infrastructure – where governments are expected to be the main financier, shouldering around 90% of the needed finance – and hard infrastructure such as transportation systems, ports, energy systems, and telecommunications, which the private sector can finance in the range of 60-80%. The latter boils down to roughly 500 to 700 billion US $ – a colossal amount of money.

CRUCIAL CONNECTORS

We can compare the role of banks to that of a hub-and-spoke system used in the airline industry: the bank forms the hub of a network of companies, each of which are connected to the bank through the latter's role as investor. Being the hub allows a bank to influence the focus and behaviour of these companies through frequent contact and by setting out investment conditions with regard to sustainable business.

Large institutional investors such as pension funds and insurance companies have the potential to influence entire sectors through their investment decisions, as we are now seeing in the decline of the coal and oil sectors. That is one of main reasons why FMO focuses almost 50% of its business on the financial sector. Simply put, this is where we feel we can make a difference – by opening up access to financial services in underserved countries, by providing access to credit for small and medium-sized enterprises, and by helping banks to focus on sustainable business and to apply international standards on human rights and social and environmental issues. It is heartening to see that, after focusing on these issues over the last decade, FMO is seeing more and more of its clients becoming leaders in their national industries with regard to environmental and social standards.

RESPONSIBLE RISK-TAKERS

I frequently hear complaints that banks are reluctant to take risks and that pension funds are too risk averse. This may be true, but the flip side is that when financial institutions take significant amounts of risk, this might lead to unacceptable losses. I don't think that most people would like to hear from their bank or their pension fund that it took too much risk on financing the Global Goals and that therefore their pension will unfortunately be lower or their deposit can't be returned. More pertinently, we all witnessed in 2008 what happens when banks take on too much risk.

In banking, risk primarily refers to the chance that the borrower will not repay his/her loan or that you will sell your equity stake at a loss. Let me illustrate this with an example. Say a bank has a portfolio of 100 loans at €10 each and it charges a 1% interest rate to offset the risk. To cover the risk of the entire portfolio, therefore, the bank has (1% for the risk) x (100 loans) x (€10/per loan) = €10 – the equivalent of one loan. If just one company cannot repay its loan, the banks loses €10, which is its entire margin. What this comes down to is that the risk that a bank can take is that of one in 100 loans failing. That does not leave much room for error. In the case of equity investments, the returns are higher and therefore an investor can take a higher risk. Equity is by definition a higher risk because if a company is in trouble, the borrowers will be the first to be repaid, and if there is any money left over, it goes to the equity holders. At the same time, the potential gain for equity holders is higher because they participate in the company's profits, while the gain for lenders is capped by the loan's interest rate.

I will return to this topic in a later chapter when I explain how governments and development banks can help financial institutions take higher risks without putting your savings or pensions at risk.

RESPONSIBLE INVESTORS

Most of the principles that apply to businesses pertain to investors as well. This means that investors should also define how they wish to contribute to society and put this at the core of their investing strategy. The steps required to create a sustainable business also hold for financial institutions: be profitable and transparent; measure your impact; incorporate sustainable standards; focus on fair jobs, green investments, and inclusive business; and pay appropriate taxes. What gives financial institutions extra leverage is that they can lean on their clients to also incorporate these practices into their everyday operations. DFIs have been frontrunners in this area, and their experience can be useful for other investors.

It all starts with the selection of clients and investee companies. Most financial institutions have already taken the step of defining lists that exclude certain categories of companies – such as the weapons industry – from their investment universe. The next step would be to take a proactive approach and select those companies and sectors that actively seek to achieve the Global Goals.

There is at the moment a very heated discussion taking place among investors on whether to stop investing in the coal and oil industries. For investors, the decision does not solely depend on the righteousness of investing in these sectors, it is also a question of risk management. According to the International Energy Agency, changes in consumer behaviour and the introduction of new government regulations can turn certain industries such as coal and oil into businesses that are no longer viable. From an investor's point of view, such industries are no longer interesting to invest in: they have become 'stranded assets'.*

---

* The IEA defines stranded assets as "those investments which have already been made but which, at some point prior to the end of their economic life (as assumed at the investment decision point), are no longer able to earn an economic return, as a result of changes in the market and regulatory environment".

Some time ago I was invited by a pension fund in the process of defining its new strategy to provide my view on whether investing in sustainable businesses was riskier and less profitable. I pointed out that there are studies that show that sustainable businesses perform better than their peers, but I also suggested they turn the question around: might investing in *unsustainable* businesses not be riskier and less profitable in the long run? Because that could be very well be the case in the coming decades.

Qualifying as a sustainable investor requires adhering to various international standards and particular ways of reporting. The main challenge here is to ensure that these reporting requirements and international standards are not simply tucked into a drawer and forgotten. Many organisations and companies subscribe to standards without really understanding and implementing them. Some banks simply pass the responsibility of implementing the standards on to their clients without following up. FMO tries to adapt all of these standards to the situation on the ground by discussing realistic possibilities with clients on an equal footing. We complete risk assessments with our clients and define concrete goals and targets together with them. These are then regularly monitored. In this way, we initiate an incremental process towards sustainable practices. When clients comply with the targets we have set, this lowers the risk for us, enabling us to reduce our interest rates for them.

Once sustainable business principles are integrated into the core of a company's mission, the role of the company's sustainability specialists should be integrated into core business operations as well. This is what FMO did back in 2007 when we transferred our specialists in environmental, social, and governance issues from the risk department to the commercial side of the bank, enabling them to become a part of our investment decisions from the outset. Rather than being seen an obstacle to investment and an external check, these specialists now help to select investments that meet ESG requirements from the beginning. They even assist in identifying business opportunities. With this internal transformation, we began practicing what we had preached.

Sustainable Investing

How can financial institutions persuade their clients to implement sustainable standards in a way that creates the maximum impact?

A key requisite is the aligning of the company's long-term ambitions with those of the development bank. It is not enough to say: 'If you want our money, do as we say.' That does not help anyone. Investors and the entrepreneurs they invest in must be on the same page, otherwise implementation can become a long and nasty process that fails to deliver the intended results.

In moving towards sustainability, the best way forward is to strike a balance between ambition and pragmatism. Often there are concerns about whether a project is adopting international best practices quickly enough. The mission of development banks is to help developing economies develop, which means that inevitably we work with companies where there is considerable room for improvement. In almost all cases, we step in when there is still a lot of work to be done. We therefore understand that development processes take time.

As part of ensuring their clients' success, development banks can help to improve a company's governance structures as well as its capacity to manage its social and environmental targets. Such a process can take the form of technical assistance or providing access to the network and knowledge that development banks have.

In urging our commercial banking clients to adopt sustainable banking, FMO used to focus on getting the message through to middle management in the expectation that it would permeate throughout the business. After a thorough internal reassessment, however, we decided to take a different approach: we decided to engage the management board and to see the process as a mutual learning experience. By explaining the benefits of environmental, social, and governance risks using regional examples and by engaging in a dialogue at the leadership level, the message can permeate downward throughout all levels of the business. We are then able to clearly convey that, rather than cutting into profits, ESG requirements not only mitigate risk but also generate new opportunities.

Green Investing

Green investments are an up-and-coming asset class that has been growing significantly in recent years. Green investing refers to investments in companies that facilitate a positive impact on the environment. These are becoming increasingly popular, as seen in the emergence last year of so-called green bonds* as a new asset class. Development banks have played an active role in the initial development of these markets. FMO issued the first public green and inclusive bond in the Netherlands in 2014. What these markets still lack, however, are clear and unified definitions to enable investors to actually invest in the issues they are concerned about. Besides green bonds, there are many other green investments such as green mortgages, energy efficiency schemes, renewable energy programmes, and ecological restoration projects.

Inclusive Investing

Although I will be handling this topic more extensively in chapter four, I will simply point out here that the best example of inclusive investing is microfinance. This is an industry that that has reached out to hundreds of millions of unbanked or underbanked households in emerging markets and developing economies. Outside of the microfinance field, investors and banks can and should actively look for inclusive business models that fit their risk appetite.

PARTNERING IN SUSTAINABLE DEVELOPMENT PROJECTS

Partnering is the ability to engage, the ability to understand each other's business, the ability to take on risks, and the ability to turn around at the right point in time.

– Kshama Fernandes, CEO IFMR Capital, India

There are a number of different players involved in the financing of sustainable development, each operating in their own space. Where these spaces overlap, these players can – and should – collaborate. For it is clear that financing the tremendous amount of investment needed for the changeover to sustainable development will require economies of scale, and the most effective way to achieve such scale is through partnerships.

---

* Green bonds are bonds that are used to finance projects with a positive environmental impact.

When I attended one of the yearly conferences hosted by the Clinton Global Initiative, one precept I came across that resonated with me was: "When it's not scalable, it's a hobby." I believe that only sufficiently large-scale initiatives can help us solve our worldwide issues in time. DFIs are perfectly positioned to facilitate scalability because they can take on more risk than other financial institutions. They can link governments with the private sector, mobilise funds, and demonstrate the viability of impact investing.

In the following pages, I will say a few words about the key players – in addition to development finance institutions – that finance sustainable development: impact investors, commercial banks, pension funds, and central banks.

IMPACT INVESTORS

There is as yet no uniform definition of 'impact investing'. What all impact investors do have in common is that they aim to generate a positive social and/or environmental impact through their investments. Not all impact investors expect to earn a return on their investment: there are those who do not mind making a loss on their investment, those who aim to receive their investment back without a return, and those who endeavour to receive an adequate return on their investment. In all cases, however, earning a financial return is not the main motivation for investing.

Impact investors can be individual investors – a category that includes everything from the small-time investor looking to invest his/her savings in an ethical way to the billionaire with a vision on how to make the world a better place – but the bulk of impact investors are institutional investors. The latter includes such categories as social venture capital funds; private philanthropic foundations; and non-profit, non-governmental organisations set up to pursue a specified non-financial objective.

Among those defining themselves as impact investors are so-called family offices. A family office is an investment group that is created using the profits earned by family-owned companies. Most began as charities set up with the purpose of achieving a specific social goal such as improving education or providing better access to healthcare. As the amount of capital owned by these rich families has grown over the years, so has the amount of capital managed by these foundations. Over the last decade, a number of these family offices have moved away from giving out grants, moving instead into impact investing. Among the more sizeable and well-known of these are the Bill & Melinda Gates Foundation and the Chan Zuckerberg Initiative. One association that has been active in peer-to-peer impact investing for more than 20 years already is Put Your Money Where Your Meaning Is Community (PYMWYMIC), an association of families and philanthropists who help fund companies that generate a positive impact on the planet and on people.

JPMorgan, Monitor-Deloitte, and the Calvert Foundation have estimated that impact investing will increase to between US $400 billion and US $1 trillion worldwide by 2020. Interestingly, according to JPMorgan, most commercial forms of impact investing are currently being targeted at emerging markets.

In 2009, the Rockefeller Foundation, JPMorgan, and the United States Agency for International Development created the Global Impact Investing Network (GIIN), an organised network of impact investors that is, in its own words, 'dedicated to increasing the scale and effectiveness of impact investing'. GIIN has created a taxonomy of metrics called Impact Reporting and Investment Standards (IRIS) that can be used to measure social and environmental impact. GIIN provides IRIS free of charge as part of its endeavour to enhance the consistency and reliability of impact measurement practices throughout the impact investing industry. The larger aim of GIIN is to support and stimulate the development of the impact investing market so that it functions in much the same way as traditional markets.

The emergence of impact investing in recent years has meant that development banks are no longer the sole players in financing sustainable development. There is much we can learn from each other in our differing approaches. Private foundations such as family offices are unique in that they are unregulated financial institutions. While DFIs are required to set a cap on their investment timelines in order to accurately analyse the risks involved, private foundations have the freedom to define their own investment horizons. Their autonomy also enables them to create more efficient business models – models that DFIs and other impact investors can then build on. NGOs, some of whom are also involved in impact investing, can provide expertise on the local market and often play an essential role in community engagement.

Partnerships can bring together impact investors that have complementary attributes. All financial institutions are constrained by the regulations that determine their business model, but collaboration allows them to transcend these limitations. Moreover, because each institution has a different capacity to absorb risk, there is added value in teaming up with other institutions that can take more risk. The benefit is that the savings of all the institutions in a team can be mobilised, which can then be used to finance projects that would have been too large-scale for any single institution to finance. And because each financial institution has different areas of expertise and seeks different risk profiles, they can complement one another and thereby 'catalyse' more commercial capital.

That strong parallels exist between development banks and impact investors in terms of the task we have taken upon ourselves and the objectives we have formulated is plainly evident. Although we have sprouted from different soils – the roots of development banking lie in governments and public funding, while impact investing stems from the private sector – we have grown into a common space. Impact investors bring a commercial mindset and an element of competition to the world of sustainable development that can only spur the other key players in the field to reach higher.

COMMERCIAL BANKS

There are, of course, banks that also support sustainable development by embedding it into the core of their business. In the Netherlands, Triodos and ASN are the most prominent examples. Handelsbanken in Sweden is another. And over the years, an increasing number of financial institutions in FMO's portfolio have been devoting their efforts to reducing their negative environmental impact as well as branching out into more inclusive finance.

In 2009, in the wake of the outbreak of the financial crisis, the CEO of Triodos Bank and the Chairperson of BRAC Bank in Bangladesh founded the Global Alliance for Banking on Values (GABV), which aims to promote social and environmental sustainability as well as inclusive finance within the banking system. The alliance has grown quickly and now has 28 financial institutions as members. The GABV provides a clear example of sustainable and ethical banking, and its steady growth shows that this is a viable banking model with significant growth potential. Because all members of GABV must be private retail banks, FMO is only an associate member. I do attend the GABV annual meetings, which are always a great opportunity to share experiences and ideas with other CEOs working from a different perspective but with the same beliefs and goals. Several of FMO's clients in Africa, Asia, and Latin America are GABV members.

PENSION FUNDS

From the perspective of those involved in sustainable development, pension funds represent a vast pool of untapped potential. If only a fraction of their capital was invested in sustainable business in emerging markets, that alone could significantly accelerate the transformation to a sustainable economy. FMO recognised this several years ago, and we worked for a number of years to develop an avenue through which pension funds could invest. After several attempts, we finally created a separate, licensed investment firm – FMO Investment Management (FIM) – to channel capital from institutional investors into FMO's portfolio of companies.

FMO's idea was to create private equity funds in which pension funds could invest. The private equity funds would be participating in FMO's portfolio of private equity investments. But it soon became clear that we could not find a way to get pension funds to participate.

At the same time we created a debt fund focused on loans to commercial banks that service small and medium-sized enterprises in emerging markets. Some of the smaller pension funds in the Netherlands were interested in this debt investment fund, and in 2015 we managed to close our first debt fund at €150 million. In 2016 we started a new debt fund with a Dutch commercial bank for their private clients to invest in a cross-section of FMO's portfolio. This is one of the first impact funds in which private persons can invest in a broad portfolio that is made up of more than simply microfinance institutions.

While these are important successes, DFIs have struggled to involve pension funds in their debt and equity funds on any significant scale. Based on my own experience in the Netherlands, I can identify several reasons for this. The pension fund industry in the Netherlands is very much dominated by the two largest pension funds – one with more than € 300 billion in assets under management and another with € 180 billion. The smaller pension funds – of which there are more than 50 – take their cue from the market leaders, which means that the likelihood that they will consider investing in a fund is significantly higher if one of the larger pension funds is invested in it. Another obstacle is that the larger pension funds are not very interested in investing less than € 100 million per investment fund. This often rules out sustainable investment funds, since they tend to be much smaller in scale. Moreover, the way in which the assets of these pension funds are managed makes it very complicated for DFIs to match pension funds' needs. I like to use the analogy of a puzzle box with key slots, each with a different shape and size, and the trick is to find the key that matches the slot. Too often, innovative and offbeat investments – such as those offered by FMO's investment management firm – are judged to be an improper fit.

The good news is that many pension funds have recently been giving greater priority to sustainable business. FMO will continue talking to them, exchanging views and expertise on how to incorporate sustainability in policies and in practice. It is clear that development banks such as FMO need to start working more closely with pension funds. One model that I could see becoming successful is where DFIs and pension funds co-create new funds that fit the latter's investment policies, risk profiles, and requirements in terms of governance and structure.

CENTRAL BANKS

Central bank policies are crucial to moving financial systems forward in the areas of sustainable development. They can be a key force driving financial institutions to adopt social and environmental standards and to pursue financial inclusion. In general, central banks in developing countries have been quicker to assume their responsibility for promoting sustainable economic development, while their counterparts in developed countries have only recently expanded their responsibilities beyond monitoring financial risks in the monetary system. When FMO began working in the financial sector in Nigeria, the Nigerian central bank was one of the first in the world to introduce sustainable banking principles, which its banks were required to comply with. When speaking at a conference at the Sustainable Finance Lab in the Netherlands, people thought that I had lost my mind when I told them that the Nigerian central bank was far ahead of the Dutch central bank in this area.

In addition to Nigeria, the central banks of Bangladesh, Kenya, and Brazil are also taking an active role in introducing policies to promote sustainability within their financial systems. More recently, the Bank of England has begun to take seriously the negative effects that climate change and income inequality may have on financial stability, while its Dutch counterpart is also prioritising sustainability and recognising its own responsibility in this area. If more central banks were to take on the responsibility of promoting sustainable economic development, they would accelerate the change needed in their financial sectors and in so doing greatly advance the global development movement.

CONCLUSION

I hope this chapter has made it clear that the financial sector is key to enabling the world to make great strides in sustainability. In functioning as the hub of the economy, financial institutions can – and should – support their clients in embedding sustainability into their business. connect companies seeking a loan or equity with what is needed for sustainable development. But this changeover to sustainability must first take place in-house, with environmental and social standards as well as green and inclusive finance becoming part of the core business of financial institutions. Although more players in the financial sector are now beginning to make the shift towards sustainable development and a growing number of impact investors are joining the market, the movement will not gain sufficient traction until pension funds and insurance companies are enlisted and central banks start to include sustainability in their risk assessments of national financial systems. To reach the economies of scale necessary to achieve our goals in time, development banks will need to act as the bridge between governments and businesses.

Development Banks Explained

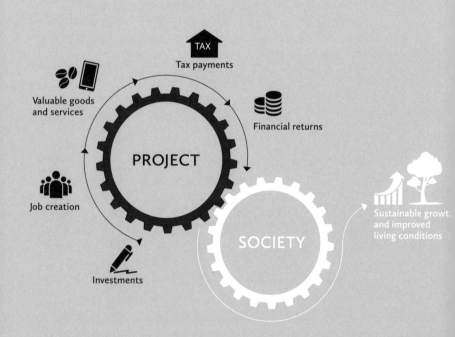

TAX
Tax payments

Valuable goods
and services

Financial returns

PROJECT

Job creation

SOCIETY

Investments

Sustainable growth
and improved
living conditions

Source: Commons Consultants, Copenhagen

THE ROLE OF DEVELOPMENT BANKS

Thus far, I have stressed the need for an integrated approach to the challenges the world faces – one that addresses the intertwined nature of poverty, inequality, climate change, loss of biodiversity, tax avoidance, and bad business practices. Rather than treating these issues as separate challenges, we must see them as symptoms of larger systemic problems and treat them as such. I have argued in chapters three and four that both businesses and the financial sector not only can but must contribute to a sustainable world.

BRIDGING BUSINESSES, THE FINANCIAL SECTOR, AND GOVERNMENTS

It is now time to delve into the world of development banks. Development finance institutions (DFIs) are a rapidly growing force that are crucial to reaching the Global Goals. They are a good example of blended finance, and they are ideal conduits for development finance because they understand and work with the sectors of government, business, and finance. This understanding allows them to distribute risks between the parties they work with in a way that fits each party's different risk model. In this chapter I want to take a look at how DFIs have helped develop the microfinance industry in developing countries, the mobile phone and private equity sectors in Africa, and finally the Environmental Social and Governance (ESG) policies used by financial institutions in Africa, Asia, and Latin America. Most of the examples I provide are projects that were financed by FMO, since these are the cases I know well.

DEVELOPMENT BANKS EXPLAINED

Development finance institutions were created to finance private companies in developing countries. When the world was focused on the Millenium Development Goals, DFIs concentrated on poverty alleviation by investing in companies that created jobs, generated tax income, and often also earned much-needed foreign currency for the country. In more recent years, environmental and social issues have become the core focus of DFIs, in particular the reduction of greenhouse gas emissions and the promotion of inclusive finance.

For the most part, DFIs are (completely or partially) government-owned companies, although their governance structure differs from country to country. All DFIs operate in developing countries on the continents of Africa, Asia, and Latin America, and some focus more on low-income countries while others more on regions. By definition, DFIs aim to be additional to the markets they work in, which means they must take on more risk than commercial parties are able (or want) to take. All DFIs target a profitable return ranging between 1% and 12%.

DFIs offer a variety of products including senior loans, equity, guarantees, and grants for technical assistance. For most DFIs, investments in the financial sector (e.g. banks, lease companies, monetary financial institutions, insurance companies) make up a significant part of their portfolios. For some of the larger DFIs, close to half of their total investments are in the financial sector. By investing in the financial sector, DFIs indirectly finances micro, small, and medium-sized companies. The second largest portion of DFIs' investment portfolio is in energy, followed by infrastructure and manufacturing. All DFIs have a special focus on the agri-food sector due to the large impact this sector has on food security and the environment. Together, DFIs have a collective investment portfolio of more than US $80 billion. The companies DFIs have invested in have created more than 4 million jobs and have contributed billions of dollars in tax income.

EUROPEAN DEVELOPMENT BANKS

More than twenty years ago, the association of European Development Finance Institutions (EDFI) was created to facilitate cooperation between the 15 bilateral development banks in Europe. The EDFI recently decided to step up its advocacy efforts in order to increase the visibility of DFIs vis-a-vis the European Union as well as in their respective home countries. In 2016, EDFI created a management company to manage funds for the EU for special purposes in the private sector. In the coming years, these funds are expected to grow and diversify into areas such as rural electrification, small farmers, forestry, and gender finance.

European DFIs often co-finance ojects whose financing needs are higher than what an individual bank can offer. Drawing from this collaborative experience, EDFI created a highly efficient co-financing vehicle between development banks called European Financing Partners in 2004. Using a common decision-making mechanism, every participant follows the leader once a decision is made – a unique mechanism that effectively aligns visions. The portfolios of all European DFIs are worth a total of €36 billion, which makes them a significant and rapidly growing actor in financing sustainable development

I was chair of the EDFI board from 2010-2013 and then again in 2015-2016 because I believe that EDFI can be an important instrument for DFIs to jointly position themselves through policy papers. The association is also an important vehicle for representing the group to the EU.

In addition to DFIs that are established by and receive funding from a single government, which are known as bilateral DFIs, there are also multilateral development banks such as the European Bank for Reconstruction and Development, which is mainly active in the former Soviet republics and Northern Africa; the International Finance Cooperation, the private sector arm of the World Bank; and the African Development Bank, the Asian Development Bank, the Inter-American Development Bank in Latin America, and the North American Development Bank established by the United States and Mexico. Bilateral and multilateral DFIs often work together in order to be able to finance sustainable development projects, thereby expanding the scale of our impact.

THE EXPERTISE OF DEVELOPMENT BANKS

Development finance institutions have valuable expertise when it comes to implementing and completing investments in sustainable development. This is expertise that all other financial players can draw on in their efforts to contribute to a better world. Below, I highlight a range of areas in which DFIs have extensive knowledge and experience.

> *It is my inherent belief that DFIs should be the ones to lead the game and be up there in terms of taking potential risks that entities who are normally not in the DFI space cannot take.*
>
> – Kshama Fernandes, CEO IFMR Capital, India

Selecting Clients

DFIs have vast experience in selecting clients from a sustainable development perspective. The ideal client is one that already has sustainability embedded in its mission, has a proven track record of achieving an impact that aligns with the impact goals of the financial institution or company, and on top of that has outstanding integrity. Because there are few potential clients in the emerging markets that meet all of these criteria, a financial institution must find the best possible balance.

DFIs have specific criteria that must be met before they choose to finance a project. As in risk analysis, each opportunity introduces a host of important questions. Is this project creating fair jobs? Is it minimising its carbon dioxide emissions? Can the client service their debt in time? Is there an option to attract other investors for this project? Is the project economically inclusive? What are the environmental, social, and governance risks, and can these standards be improved? The list is a long one. A project does not have to meet every single requirement – a development bank will consider each project within the larger context of the portfolio it aims to create.

In selecting clients, development finance institutions evaluate not only the direct impact that the company has but also its indirect impact via the company's value chain. Producers of chocolate, for example, must trace where and how the cacao they use has been produced. The same trend can be seen in the palm oil and cotton industries. It is crucial for the client to take responsibility for companies in its value chain and to define standards and limits for them.

Combining Impact and Profit

DFIs have shown again and again that sustainability impact and profit can go hand in hand. It all starts with an exhaustive assessment of the risks involved in difficult and unstable political and economic environments. Because DFIs must be additional to the market and take higher risks than the other investors in that market, the financing that DFIs provide tends to be long-term. Their knowledge, expertise, and network allow them to accurately assess the long-term risks involved. The long-term partnerships DFIs develop with their clients also generally make their interventions more effective. If we look at FMO's experience in the field as well as our ex-post evaluations, we have seen that most companies that generate a positive sustainability impact also generate an adequate return. DFIs are still quite unique in the private sector in that they measure and report on the impacts generated by their clients.

So what kind of risks does a development bank take that a commercial bank cannot? They can take more equity risks and more long-term risks in developing countries. This is quite unique. In most low-income countries, there is no access to long-term capital because there are no long-term savings. The most important source of long-term savings are pension funds and life insurance companies, and these are small if not non-existent in most of the countries we operate in. Foreign commercial banks are not willing to take long-term risk but do provide loans of up to three years in most countries. By contrast, development banks provide loans of up to fifteen years. We try to limit the company risk and in general only finance companies that have at least a three-year track record. This means they have proven that there is a market for their product, that the technology works, that they can manage a company, and so on.

Implementing Environmental and Social Standards

Incorporating an analysis of the environmental and social risks into the client relationship is a core aspect of the development bank business process. To a new client who has never considered these risks before, development banks can often appear demanding or unrealistic, but DFIs have learned to adapt their requirements to local circumstances and create, together with the client, an incremental process towards the best sustainable practices. Over time, it becomes clear that these standards are integral to the client's long-term success. It can take months or sometimes even years before they begin to appreciate the value added by the adequate management of environmental and social risks, standards, and values.

Applying international standards on social, environmental, and human rights issues is a continuous learning experience. Though DFIs have the broad expertise to apply these standards in different sectors, countries, and circumstances, they are still learning to work together with partners such as NGOs in these areas.

Mobilising your Network

Development banks can use their 'power to convene' to unite and bring other financial organisations together to establish sustainable industry standards from within the financial sector in a given country.

Our clients often point out that our requirement that they incorporate environmental and social standards into their business puts them at a disadvantage vis-a-vis their competitors. To even out the playing field in this regard, we have initiated what we call sector initiatives designed to introduce ESG standards to entire sectors. FMO has so far developed ESG sector initiatives in Paraguay, Nigeria, Mongolia, Bangladesh, Vietnam, and Kenya. In this section, I want to examine the cases of Paraguay and Nigeria to demonstrate how this worked.

Honestly my first thought, was 'Oh God, he's setting the bar high! How are we going to comply with that?' We went from surprise, panic, to understanding, and finally went to working on this challenge.

– Connor McEnroy, Chairman Sudameris, Paraguay

Convincing Paraguay of the Importance of Sustainability

In 2009, FMO began assessing whether it should begin investing in Paraguay – one of the poorer countries in South America and one whose economy is heavily dependent on agricultural production. Paraguay is home to one of the continent's last remaining expanses of relatively intact nature known as the Chaco. This vast mix of grasslands and forest is quickly shrinking as a result of government policies focused on boosting the competitiveness of the Paraguayan cattle and agricultural sectors, which allowed farmers to exploit the area for cattle ranching and farming purposes. FMO decided to begin investing cautiously and to keep a watchful eye on sustainability standards. In our conversations with the banks we financed, we quickly ran into a deadlock on the subject of adhering to international environmental standards. Once the banks understood what adherence to international standards meant, they refused to sign because they knew that what the standards entailed was not something they could achieve in their local context in the short or even medium term.

We explored a step-by-step approach and developed a country strategy that was based on focusing in the first place on compliance with the local law, which in the Paraguayan context of a powerless and under-resourced environmental agency would in itself be a huge improvement to the status quo. Banks hold immense sway in the country, and if we could mobilise them as an entire industry to comply with local environmental decrees we were convinced that the environmental impact would be enormous. If compliance with the local law was achieved, we could then work towards fulfilling international standards through steady incremental improvements.

In order to overcome our clients' concern that strict environmental requirements would drive away their clients, we gathered together all of our bank clients in Paraguay to try to convince them to take part in a collective push for the same standards. It was clear that this had to be done at the board level and that we had to bring the shareholders of the different banks into contact with one another. I therefore travelled to Paraguay in 2012 and invited the board members for a dinner conversation on sustainability. Because I have lived in Latin America for ten years and can speak the language, I can connect to FMO's clients in Latin America more easily and more deeply than any other region of the world. Connecting on a cultural level in that way naturally creates a mutual understanding. Over dinner with four executives of Paraguayan banks, I tried to begin a conversation on sustainability, stressing the value it can add for them and for their clients in the long term. The topic was clearly new and uncomfortable, and I felt as though I was making little if any progress. We made our way through the evening, through dessert even, without a response to my attempts to broach the subject. I was worried that we would run out of time when suddenly one of the CEOs stood up and said, "If the CEO of FMO has come all the way to Paraguay to talk about sustainability, it must be important to him. As we are his clients, we should listen to him to understand why it is important for us." That was exactly the leg up that I needed.

After that, the board members agreed to have FMO take the first step by exploring sustainability within their respective risk departments. Using that opening, FMO then began to work intensively with these banks to explore ways to comply with the local law. I made it a precondition to involve national and international NGOs. I was convinced that we really could make a difference in Paraguay. But if we went in alone on this, it would be impossible to generate enough impact. We needed others to confirm that our work was useful and that it would make the difference that was needed.

With our approach of moving ahead one small step at a time but insisting rather relentlessly that these steps be implemented – combined with ongoing, intensive engagement and support – we made credible progress, and a legitimate story for further investment began to take shape. Since the official launch of the roundtable in 2012, the size of the table has grown to eight banks, which together represent more than three-quarters of the commercial finance market. Together the banking industry is now designing a set of specific standards for different sectors that will raise the bar for all clients of the financial sector.

Culture change happens through people. In Paraguay, FMO was able to create a core group of bankers who understand and are committed to sustainability standards. As a result, their loan officers are now aware of them. Because we understand that implementing standards is far from easy, especially at the start, we now take the time and the energy to support our clients. By producing champions, you create a culture that perpetuates itself.

The key lesson here is that private markets and sectors can take the initiative and set new standards without a government mandate. When DFIs and their clients work together in a united and coordinated push, we can create new and effective solutions to structural issues within markets. By engaging everyone, we establish collective responsibility. If built on the proper foundations, these shifts can gain traction and begin to build on one another, allowing sustainability to gain momentum. Banks can truly become levers for creating a better world. As neutral conveners, DFIs can build bridges between banks at the local level, creating sustainable impact at the sector level and at the same time making the entire sector more attractive for investors.

> *Implementing environmental and social standards: I knew it was the right thing to do. But how to survive when my competitors don't do the same – it appeared impossible at times.*
>
> – Herbert Wigwe, CEO Access Bank, Nigeria

Implementing Sustainable Development Standards in Nigeria

Environmental and Social Standards in the Nigerian Financial Sector
FMO faced a similar issue in Nigeria – a country whose dependence on oil and gas is expensive and taxing on the environment. Nigeria's banking market is one of the largest financial sectors in Africa and also highly competitive. It therefore came as no surprise to us that Nigerian banks were also reluctant to put themselves at a competitive disadvantage as the first movers in implementing environmental and social standards. It was clear to them that such an endeavour would take time and moreover exclude clients that are unable or unwilling to meet them. Why would a bank want to limit their client base when none of its competitors were doing so?

In 2010, we met with four other development banks – IFC, DEG, the African Development Bank, and Proparco – to discuss this issue. We invited their commercial investment managers as well as their sustainability specialists for what would be the first time that they had collectively assembled from around the world. After a day of discussions, we agreed on to undertake three things: 1) to conduct collective training of Nigerian bankers, 2) to collect relevant case studies on how sustainability affects a business's bottom line, and 3) to conduct a CEO roundtable. We needed to bring the decision-makers together in order to solve these issues. In March 2011, we started the training. Access Bank pointed out almost immediately that we had never demonstrated why they should care. We returned with a cost-benefit analysis to convince management that if they do not address environmental and social standards now, they will pay the price in the future. Our message was clear: upholding environmental and social standards

BANKERS' COMMITTEE

JOINT STATEMENT OF COMMITMENT BY MEMBERS OF THE BANKERS COMMITTEE

"THE NIGERIAN SUSTAINABLE BANKING PRINCIPLES"

As leaders in the Nigerian financial sector, we are uniquely positioned to further economic growth and development in Nigeria through our regulatory, lending and investment activities across a diversity of segments and sectors of the Nigerian economy. The context in which we make business decisions is, however, characterized by complex and growing challenges relating to population growth, urban migration, poverty, destruction of biodiversity and ecosystems, pressure on food sources, prices and security, lack of energy and infrastructure and potential climate change legislation from our trade partners, amongst others.

Increasingly, it has been demonstrated that the development imperative in Nigeria should not only be economically viable, but socially relevant and environmentally responsible. We recognize that we have a role and responsibility to deliver positive development impacts to society whilst protecting the communities and environments in which we operate – for today's generation as well as for future generations. We believe that such an approach, one of sustainable banking, is consistent with our individual and collective business objectives, and can stimulate further economic growth and opportunity as well as enhance innovation and competitiveness.

Given the above considerations, we are prepared to take steps to ensure that our business decision-making activities take these considerations into account and are, where applicable, consistent with relevant international standards and practices, but with due regard for the Nigerian context and distinct development needs.

Consequently, we hereby state our commitment to developing and launching a voluntary set of Nigerian sustainable banking principles which will include:

1) An over-arching set of guidelines relating to our: (a) direct impact on communities and the environment as a result of our own business operations; and (b) indirect impacts on communities and the environment as a result of our lending and investment activities;

2) A set of sector-specific guidelines, including as a first priority: (a) oil and gas; (b) power (with a focus on renewable energy); and (c) agriculture and related water resource issues;

3) A commitment to raising awareness and developing meaningful and lasting local capacity to manage emerging environmental and social risks and opportunities within our internal operations, as well as to relevant financial sector government agencies, learning institutions and service providers.

In developing these sustainable banking principles, we recognize the need for a process which involves the engagement of relevant stakeholders and industry experts. We also recognize the need for an approach which provides for appropriate levels of transparency, accountability and self-assessment through regular reporting to our stakeholders. We will seek to work with the Central Bank of Nigeria, other relevant government agencies and development finance institutions to create the enabling environment as well as the incentives and enforcement mechanisms required for successful adoption and uptake of the sustainable banking principles.

We acknowledge that we can better support environmentally and socially responsible economic development in Nigeria by joining forces rather than standing alone. We hereby sign this Joint Commitment Statement with the aim of developing a set of sustainable banking principles for the Nigerian banking sector, to drive long-term sustainable growth whilst focusing on development priorities, safeguarding the environment and our people, and delivering measurable benefits to society and the real economy.

SIGNATORIES

Sanusi Lamido Sanusi
Central Bank of Nigeria

Umaru Ibrahim
Nigeria Deposit Insurance Corporation

Tunde O. Lemo
Central Bank of Nigeria

Suleiman Barau
Central Bank of Nigeria

Sarah O. Alade
Central Bank of Nigeria

Kingsley Moghalu
Central Bank of Nigeria

Aigboje Aig-Imoukhuede
Access Bank Plc

Emeka Emuwa
Citi Bank Nigeria Limited

Alex Otti
Diamond Bank Plc

Jibril Aku
Ecobank Plc

Ahmed Kuru
Enterprise Bank Ltd

Gbenga Alofoyun
Equatorial Trust Bank Ltd

Ladi Balogun
First City Monument Bank Plc

Reginald Ihejiahi
Fidelity Bank Plc

Suzanne Iroche
Finbank Plc

Stephen Olabisi Onasanya
First Bank of Nigeria Plc

Segun Agbaje
Guaranty Trust Bank Plc

Victor Etuokwu
Intercontinental Bank Plc

Otti Bonone
Keystone Bank Ltd

Faith Tuedor-Matthews
Mainstreet Bank Ltd

John Aboh
Oceanic Bank Plc

Nebolisa Diorakeze-Etisi
Skye Bank Plc

Sola David-Borha
Stanbic IBTC Bank Plc

Bola Adesola
Standard Chartered Bank Nigeria Ltd

Razack Adeyemi Adeola
Sterling Bank Plc

Phillips Oduoza
United Bank of Africa Plc

Funke Osibodu
Union Bank of Nigeria Plc

Ado Wanka
Unity Bank of Nigeria Plc

Segun Olukanyui
Wema Bank Plc

Godwin Emefiele
Zenith Bank Plc

Abubakar Jimoh
Associated Discount House Ltd

Adaleke Shittu
Consolidated Discounts Ltd

Koredi Sagoe
Express Discount Ltd

Rilwan Belo-Osagie
First Securities Discount House Ltd

Laoye Jaiyeola
Kakawa Discount House Ltd

simply makes business sense. That was an essential turning point for both Access Bank and for the process as a whole. By September, Access Bank – with its substantial legitimacy and credibility in the sector – was playing a central role in the roundtable discussions. The banks recommended that we approach the central bank. The central bank governor, Sanusi Sanusi, was a very powerful man, and if he agreed to change the status quo, we knew that the industry would have to follow. When we asked him to join the roundtable, he declared that his first priority was economic growth – in itself not very encouraging. Nonetheless, he did agree to attend the roundtable.

I remember that we were nervous on the day of the meeting. Sanusi had just returned from China where he had met with his counterpart. In opening the discussion, Sanusi shared with us the lesson he had learned from the Chinese, which was that because they had failed to address environmental and social standards from the start, they were now paying hundreds of billions of dollars to address the consequences. He was not going to make the same mistake. At that meeting, eight banks agreed to work together on this. A committee was formed to begin implementation, and a subcommittee of the central bank dedicated solely to sustainability issues was created. Later that year, a joint statement was issued by twenty-four banks that had signed an agreement on sustainable practice. The banks then began to develop guidelines for the oil and gas, construction, and agricultural industries. In this way, the financial sector helped to design and develop regulatory guidelines, together with the central bank subcommittee on sustainability, which were then circulated by the central bank.

Implementing Corporate Governance Practices

I have not touched upon the importance of corporate governance in sustainable finance. Corporate governance is the system of rules, practices, and processes by which a company is directed and controlled. Much of the interest in corporate governance these days involves balancing the interests of the many stakeholders in a company, including shareholders, management, customers, the government, financiers, and local communities. Flawed corporate governance practices have in recent times been the cause of scandals at such corporations as Enron, Ahold, and WorldCom. In many countries there is a best-practice corporate governance code for companies trading on the stock exchange.

A significantly high number of FMO's investment write-offs – when clients cannot repay their loans – are due to bad corporate governance. It is therefore crucial for DFIs to understand and analyse a client's ownership and succession structure and the checks and balances in place at the highest echelons of the company, and then determine how to improve it. Development banks support their investee companies by improving their corporate governance – for example by calling for the appointment of a certain number of independent supervisory board members in order to introduce more viewpoints than only those of insiders such as family members.

Development banks finance many family-owned companies where succession issues and the involvement of the family in decision-making play an important role. Planning for succession can be a delicate issue, and an independent third party such as a DFI can be very helpful and effective in such matters.

Developing Projects from an Early Stage

Development banks have become increasingly involved in project development in recent years due to the lack of bankable projects in developing economies. In fields such as renewable energy, inclusive finance, off-grid energy, and financing for small farmers, there are simply not enough bankable proposals. With their technical assistance money and their long-term view, development banks are better positioned than other banks to join a project at an early stage and support the creation of bankable business models. Once a project moves further into the planning stages, finding financing ceases to be an issue.

CATALYSING EXTERNAL CAPITAL

In order to accelerate the pace at which we are moving towards the Global Goals, we need to channel more funding into investment opportunities. While the money is in truth available, what is lacking is the risk-taking capacity. Banks and investors such as pension funds have a limited risk capacity, as I explained in the previous chapter, because government regulation and the sheer responsibility of looking after the savings of many households do not give them much room to take higher risks. Development banks can reduce the risk of a project for other investors so that they can be included. They have the network, the knowledge, and the expertise to deliver solutions.

Complementing Commercial Investors

Development banks must demonstrate that they add something to a financing deal that other financial players cannot provide. This concept is known as additionality. In the case of FMO, additionality entails that we finance high-risk projects and companies that are unable to find adequate commercial investors because they are too risky, because of the long-term investment needed, or because the project or company is new to a particular market, sector, or country. There are two aspects to our additionality: we provide long-term finance where none is available, and we add value to our clients in such areas as ESG and risk management.

While FMO may finance a project on its own if size allows, the intention is always for the project to mature and become commercially bankable over time. Our aim is to support businesses so that they can eventually access commercial lenders. Development banks provide the initial foothold from which these businesses can eventually become financially independent from us.

Mobilising Financiers as Co-Investors

When development finance institutions mobilise financiers as co-investors, this is known as catalysation. In practice, a DFI will first identify and approve a project before approaching potential investors if necessary. While DFIs work within a network of investors, their involvement signals to other parties that the project is bankable and that it meets environmental, social, and governance standards. This often sparks interest from outside investors. Catalysation enhances DFIs' effectiveness: when they are able to involve third parties in their financing arrangements, DFIs' ability to generate impact as a single source of capital grows, as does the total funding in emerging markets.

The additionality that a DFI provides can vary in degree, of course. If we were to imagine a spectrum of additionality, one extreme would be the truly innovative, high-risk project that fails to generate catalysation, as the risk is simply too high for commercial investors. The other end of the spectrum would be a market that is safe enough for everyone to invest

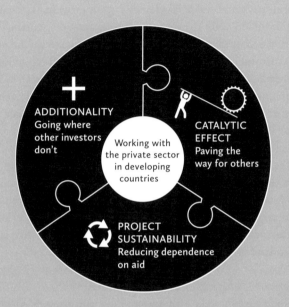

ADDITIONALITY
Going where other investors don't

CATALYTIC EFFECT
Paving the way for others

Working with the private sector in developing countries

PROJECT SUSTAINABILITY
Reducing dependence on aid

Investing in underserved geographies sectors, and segments by taking a long-run approach that permits higher risks.

Mobilising other investors by sharing risk, being first-movers demonstrating to other investors how to invest in high risk projects, and by sharing expertise.

Helping build sustainable sources of jobs and tax income by investing in financially self-sustainable projects, and by applying responsible business standards for environmental, social and governance concerns.

Source: Commons Consultants, Copenhagen

in and one in which development banks no longer have a role. When development banks want to catalyse commercial investors, they need to focus on operating somewhere in between these two extremes.

DFIs must look at what levels of risk are acceptable to commercial third parties and then determine strategies to bring down these risks so that commercial lenders are able to participate. This can be achieved at the level of a specific project, but the risks can also be reduced by diversifying the overall portfolio of investments for the commercial lender. FMO uses both strategies in different ways. FMO has projects in over 80 countries and as a result is less vulnerable to any kind of negative shock in a single country. If one country suffers, this tends to be offset by another country. Having a diversified portfolio allows us to mitigate financial risk because one failure is not automatically connected to another. This can provide a model for investors beginning in impact investment. As mentioned above, our investment management company FIM makes it possible for pension funds and also private investors to invest in a cross-section of FMO's portfolio.

Another way in which DFIs can mobilise commercial financiers is by providing a long-term loan but allowing third-party investors to provide a shorter loan. In this way, catalysed investors can avoid the higher risk of a long-term loan but still benefit from the expertise and knowledge that a development bank provides.

And finally, development banks catalyse additional financing by funding a project's initial development period – the phase with the highest risk in the development timeline. For example, FMO will finance stage one of a biogas electricity plant on Lake Kivu in Rwanda that will increase the national electricity supply by 20%, all the while removing and processing a dangerous methane gas pocket trapped under the water of the lake. Commercial financiers will step in after the completion of stage one and invest in an expansion of the plant in subsequent stages. By taking on the more risk-prone first stage and providing the expertise and technical assistance necessary to establish a stable basis for the business, development banks can lower the risk to a level appropriate for commercial investors.

Blended Finance

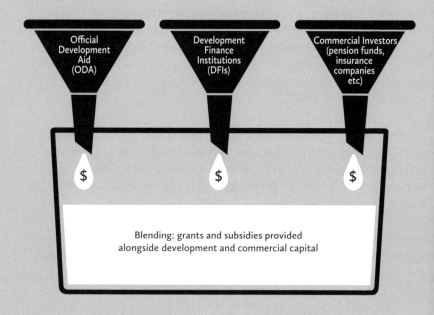

Official Development Aid (ODA)

Development Finance Institutions (DFIs)

Commercial Investors (pension funds, insurance companies etc)

$

$

$

Blending: grants and subsidies provided alongside development and commercial capital

Development banks must play to their inherent strengths that allow them to be additional and thereby create the ideal environment for commercial financiers to step in. Whether by agreeing to do the legwork and securing the initial stages of development or by allowing co-financiers the flexibility to take on the risks they can handle, a balance requires that we search for areas where our abilities overlap rather than where they diverge.

Development Banks as Instruments of Blended Finance

As I have argued in earlier chapters, we can only realise the SDGs with the involvement of private investors. Private investors can take a certain amount of financial risk but in order to scale up their investments, they need others to take on the higher risks in a transaction (or a fund). This is where blended finance can play a role: it uses public or charitable funds to reduce the level of risk in a transaction which then enables private money to flow to places and projects that they usually shun. According to the World Economic Forum, every dollar of public money invested through blended finance vehicles attracts a further US $1 to US $20 dollars in private investments.

Blending can take a number of different forms. A model often used is the three-layered fund. In this set-up, the first tranche is used in the event of losses and is financed by government ODA, the second tranche is funded by development banks, while the third tranche represents the lowest risk and therefore can be financed by private investors. Another form of blended finance is where the private investor's return is enhanced. One example is the climate fund created by the Danish development finance institution IFU. Despite the fund's higher risk level, IFU was able to accommodate the risk-return profile of the Danish pension fund that invested in it by offering a preferred return.

Blended finance can also take the form of grants for technical assistance, which help to reduce the implementation risk for commercial investors. Once the implementation risks are identified – e.g. technical knowledge, financial risk management, environmental and social risks – a programme to support the implementation can be created.

Another example of blending is one in which the total costs of developing or investing in a project are reduced through government financing. This not only reduces the investment risk but may also enhance the return for commercial investors.

Social impact bonds, which are normally emitted by (local) governments, are a specific kind of blended finance. The bonds align at least three distinct parties – the government, a service provider, and investors – around the delivery of a pre-agreed set of outcomes for an agreed financial value. For developing economies, such bonds are referred to as development impact bonds.

In blended finance, governments can reduce certain risks by providing guarantees to investors. For example, the government might guarantee long-term offtake agreements (the guaranteed buying of energy) in the case of a government-owned energy distribution company.

A major challenge with regard to blended finance is ensuring that subsidies do not result in market distortion. By offering lower-than-market-rate interest rates, blended finance could crowd out investment by commercial investors and even DFIs, as the latter also require market returns. Given that DFIs have always been required to operate under the condition of being additional to the market and to refrain from distorting the market, their experience in avoiding market distortions come in handy in deploying blended finance.

DFIs already have considerable experience in setting up blended finance vehicles, and they can function as the honest and independent broker for blending. Because of their capital structure, they can take risks that are higher than their commercial counterparts and partner with those who bring different expertise and risk-taking capabilities to the table. DFIs have built up considerable know-how on structuring financial arrangements for infrastructure projects or projects to increase inclusion. They are themselves a form of blending: when investing in private companies, they are, in fact, blending government money with private sector money. DFIs are in constant contact with their main stakeholder and shareholder – the government. They understand their government's objectives and rationale. At the same time, DFIs work closely with the private sector and understand the motivations and objectives of the business world. They are thus well-placed to bring together the different parties – each with their own 'language' and risk appetite.

Over the last year, several new platforms have emerged that aim to close the funding gap by bringing together different parties interested in investing in emerging markets and developing economies. The Sustainable Development Investment Partnership (SDIP) aims to mobilise US $100 billion for infrastructure projects in the coming five years. The Global Infrastructure Facility of the World Bank has a similar goal. Convergence is a virtual platform that facilitates blended finance by listing investment opportunities from credible investors and financiers and by streamlining the process, which reduces risks and increases returns.

Reducing Local Currency Risk for Emerging Markets

In 1987, one of FMO's clients, a credit cooperative in Peru took me out to dinner. When paying the bill, he commented that the cost of the dinner was equal to the remainder of the cooperative's loan. It was one of the first loans I had worked on when I joined FMO. Working for the Small Enterprise Department was to be a valuable learning experience for me. Given our lack of knowledge and expertise, we had to begin from the basics such as how to properly price a loan to small companies. In the case of the Peruvian credit cooperative, we had set a fixed interest rate of 4%, but then Peru fell into a financial crisis. With hyperinflation of more than 1,000% per year, the local currency became worthless, as did our loan, which meant that one dinner was enough to cover the entire loan. From then on, we only charged variable interest rates linked to existing local interest rates. Although we were to confront many such hard lessons over the years, FMO has managed to use the government contribution of ten million guilders per year (the equivalent of €4.5 million) to build up a strong portfolio of loans and equity today that is worth more than €500 million.

In 1987, the Dutch government and FMO created the Small Enterprise Fund which lends in local currency to banks that provide loans to small enterprises. This was unheard of at the time, as international development banks had always lent in dollars or other stable currencies, essentially saddling their clients with the currency risk. We felt this had to change, given that the revenues earned by almost all micro and small enterprises are in local currency. If a business received a loan of US $1,000 and the local currency then devalued by 100%, the business would have to pay back twice the amount of its original loan with interest. These are costs that can bankrupt a company.

At the time of the fund's launch, everyone in the development finance world expected the fund to lose money given the volatile nature of these local currencies. But the fund caught nearly everyone by surprise by managing not only to survive but also to make a return of 1-2% some eight years after its launch. Bigger development banks began visiting us to learn from our experience, but after conducting a fund assessment they concluded that the success of the fund could not be replicated because, according to them, it was based on pure luck. While we had already started looking for commercial and private investors to participate in the fund, our efforts were unsuccessful.

TCX, Financing in Local currency

By 2006, a few creative investment officers at FMO were convinced that we now had the experience and the track record to take the fund further. They contacted a renowned risk management consultant to help them build an economic model for a local currency fund. What they found was that if you invested in more than 20 to 25 different currencies spread over different continents, the devaluation of some currencies would offset the appreciation of others over time and that moreover a return of about 3-4% should be possible. A year later, FMO had managed to mobilise ten development banks from around the world to invest in a new fund called The Currency Exchange Fund (TCX), for roughly US $500 million.

TCX was made possible by blending grants from the Dutch and the German governments with money from development banks, commercial banks, and impact investors. Without government support, it would not have been possible for us to raise more than € 500 million and cover for more than € 3 billion in transactions. That was the start of a unique new business based on FMO's experiences with the Small Enterprise Fund.

Despite having been launched just before the outbreak of the global financial crisis, we have seen the investment portfolio suffer no more than a slight loss. The model has been put to the test again and again and has proven itself to be solid, showing that a joint effort between development banks around the world can create new transformative business models.

EXAMPLES OF SCALABLE BUSINESS MODELS

Development banks played an important role in the rise of the mobile phone industry in Africa at the end of the last century. When mobile phones were just beginning to make inroads into the African market, however, I remember there were profound doubts about whether the development community should finance their distribution. At the time, the mobile phone was seen as a luxury good and a status symbol, and many felt it would be ethically wrong to finance Africans' purchase of them if it meant they would then have less to spend on basic needs. We now know that the mobile phone completely changed the way of doing business in Africa by bringing banking services, price information, and more to people living in remote areas. I am sure this technology, especially the smartphone, will continue to be instrumental in creating new business models for those at the bottom of the pyramid

Leapfrogging to Mobile Phones

Mo Ibrahim founded Celtel in Africa in 1998, the first mover in this market. At that time, most people on the continent lacked the means to communicate across the immense distances between villages. Given the impracticality of building a serious network of landline telephones in Africa, mobile phones appeared to be the solution. However, the continent's terrible reputation for corruption, war, and dictatorships – combined with the telecommunications bust right after the "dot.com" crash in 2000 – made it almost impossible for Ibrahim to find financing. Development banks including FMO played a fundamental role in supporting Celtel with the necessary equity.

The Story of Celtel

Celtel has become a model of sustainability and a paragon for African business. Ibrahim insisted from the very beginning that he would not tolerate corruption in his business. It soon became widely known that Celtel refused to pay bribes, and many simply stopped asking the company to pay up. He insisted on doing business only with governments that utilised a transparent tender process in granting mobile telephony licenses. Within Celtel itself, every check above € 30,000 had to be approved by the board as a preventive measure. Most of Celtel's success came down to its strong governance. Ibrahim occupied only one seat on the management board, and the rest were independent directors – high-level

businesspeople in the telecom industry from all over the world. While he himself
owned more than 50% of the company, 15% of the company's shares were owned
by employees. When the company was sold to a Kuwaiti telecom company for
US $3.5 billion in 2005, all employees shared in the profit, and many actually
became millionaires. With the profits he earned from this sale, Ibrahim created
a foundation that aims to bring about meaningful change in Africa by providing
the tools to support progress in leadership and governance.

Scaling Microfinance in Emerging Markets

Development banks have been key players in the buildup of the global
microfinance industry. When I began at FMO in 1987 at the Small
Enterprise Department, our focus was on small businesses that lacked
sufficient access to credit. While we were mainly supporting government-
owned institutions that targeted these small businesses, we noticed a surge
in the number of savings and credit cooperatives that were being launched
in the 1990s. These cooperatives were essentially what we would today
call microfinance institutions. Following the lead of Grameen Bank in
Bangladesh, many NGOs began setting up such cooperatives with the
aim of providing financial services to the poor.

As development banks' mission precluded the financing of non-profit
organisations, Microfinance Institutions (MFIs) first had to become
institutions with shareholders. Development banks have helped MFIs
realise their growth potential by supporting them with technical
assistance, equity investments, and loans, thereby contributing in the early
stages to the industry's development. As competition has increased and
profit maximisation became tempting, various development banks have
used their influence to help MFIs avoid mission drift on the one hand
and on the other to implement consumer protection principles.

The microfinance industry has experienced several setbacks in recent
years as a result of MFI failures, government interventions such as in
India, and the 2008 global financial crisis, which in turn prompted an
outflow of commercial capital. DFIs have helped MFIs to ride out these
crises by supporting them financially.

The microfinance industry has grown rapidly over the last twenty years
and is now worth more than US $50 billion worldwide. Many MFIs have

been able to attract commercial funding because of the success that development banks have demonstrated with their earlier investments. Recently, several MFIs have even gone to the stock exchange to raise additional funding, allowing some early investors to earn impressive returns.

Building a Bank in Cambodia

In 1999, we began working with ACLEDA in Cambodia. At the time they approached us, ACLEDA was a small microfinance NGO. They quickly understood that if one development bank would invest in them, others would follow. Cambodia, however, was too politically unstable to be interesting to foreign investors: there had just been a coup two years earlier, and as recently as 1992 – one year before ACLEDA began – there had been no national currency. There were no regulations to speak of, and the central bank was just beginning to find its feet. Nonetheless, with our eye on the long term, we took the risk. Together with DEG, IFC, and Triodos Bank, we started to invest in ACLEDA. The investment was structured in such a way that all the parties involved – the NGO and the development banks – had the right to appoint board members. By being embedded into the governance of the institution, the development banks including FMO were able to bring their experience to the table.

What began as a credit and deposit operation – with simple savings booklets with which customers could deposit a few dollars at a time – quickly caught on. After three years, ACLEDA went from being a specialised bank to a full-fledged commercial bank in 2003. It began to branch out throughout the country and then beyond its borders into Laos and Cambodia. It even created its own banking academy. When FMO stepped in to invest just under US $500,000 in 2000, the bank's total capital was US $4 million. Now it totals US $265 million, and ACLEDA is the country's largest bank servicing 400,000 clients. They are one of the largest tax contributors of the country. The bank has undertaken many initiatives to support and train entrepreneurs as well as implement corporate governance practices, environmental and social standards, and client protection principles.

FMO eventually sold its shares in 2011 to regional commercial investors. Our task had been completed: we had seen the institution through to financial maturity and stability, and by the time we stepped out it had become a resilient and robust industry leader.

There is no doubt that microfinance has helped to lift millions of people out of extreme poverty and extended banking services to millions. The world has taken note. Commercial banks such as Citibank, Rabobank, and Deutsche Bank now have impact investing funds that have worked with MFIs for years now. However, our work is far from over, especially in Africa and Asia where there are still untold numbers of unbanked people. While microfinance has certainly proven to be a powerful tool within the broader framework of financial inclusion, I believe it would be unwise to romanticise microfinance as the one-stop solution. Although micro-entrepreneurs are given the tools to earn income for themselves, they lack the security over time that a stable job can offer. With interest rates of 30% or even 50% per loan, it is almost impossible to accumulate savings or increase their income. While these rates are better than those offered by loan sharks who demand 10% per day or week, the challenge for MFIs is to be able to lower their interest rate by lowering their operational costs. New technologies that reduce the delivery costs and cost of payment should support that change. If we want to lift people out of poverty, we must do more than simply provide them with access to financial services. Microfinance is a powerful tool with the potential to empower entrepreneurs, but in order to eliminate poverty, we need to go one step further and provide those at the bottom of the pyramid with basic services.

Financing Economic Growth through Private Equity

In 1995, FMO was one of the first development banks to step into the private equity industry in Africa, where we started supporting first-time fund managers. Private equity in Africa is another clear case of the crucial role that development banks have played in creating the industry. Development banks have traditionally been cornerstone investors in African private equity. Their investments now make up approximately 9% of total private equity investment on the continent, while this share was more than 50% when private equity in Africa first had its start. By supporting African private equity, development banks have provided small and medium-sized enterprises with access to capital, enabling economic growth from the bottom up.

Development banks have also been instrumental in fostering an emphasis on environmental, social, and governance standards among private equity funds. Historically, they have favoured funds managed by local firms or by international managers with local offices because of their goal of promoting the sustainability of local economies and the private equity industry in Africa. Development banks serve as enablers by helping to attract and mobilise private capital investment, particularly in private equity fundraising in Africa. Their role also extends to institutional capacity building. They not only upgrade social and governance practices but also help mobilise private sector financing in African states, stimulating economic development across the continent. The African private equity industry, which was virtually non-existent in 1995, has since grown into an industry worth between three and four billion dollars of investments per year.

> *The ability really to be frank, to put everything on the table, as you are confident that you will not be judged on your wild idea, is extremely important.*
>
> – Aziz Mebarek, Founding Partner AfricInvest, Tunisia

A Homegrown Private Equity Fund in Africa

In 1993, FMO was approached by three young entrepreneurs from Tunisia with little if any experience with private equity. Aziz Mebarek, Ziad Oueslati, and Karim Trad had all worked in complementary areas (industrial company, banking, audit), and now saw an opportunity to introduce private equity to their country. At the time, there were only three or four private equity funds on the entire continent, and they were all located in South Africa. The three men recognised that private equity funded locally had a future in Tunisia, where most of the banking sector was only serving multinational companies, large locally based companies, and mortgages, and where SMEs did not have sufficient access to finance. FMO recognised their vision and decided to pay to send them to SIPAREX, a private equity company in France, for six months for training in private equity. An investment of 40,000 guilders can go a long way.

One year later, the three young Tunisians set up their firm under the name of Tuninvest and started their first private equity fund in which FMO invested 0.5 million guilders. The first investments were in a chicken farm, a yoghurt factory, and other local consumer products that gave the local low-income population increased access to products and services. From the very beginning, high ethical standards were introduced, and it was made clear that both the firm and its investee companies would have nothing to do with corruption.

Building off of the success of their first fund, the group soon expanded their operations by starting a second fund covering Tunisia, Morocco, and Algeria. Their reasoning was that a business that was successful in any of these three countries should be able to succeed in the others. This second fund closed over € 120 million. In Morocco, Tuninvest helped build enterprises in a variety of sectors. At the time, Algeria was considered a very difficult market to crack. Undeterred, Tuninvest's fund sponsored the first independent leasing operation in Algeria which was to serve SMEs. FMO took an equity stake in this operation, which became very successful. The fund also backed the impressive growth of a strong local brand called Rouiba in the juice industry. Mebarek joined Roubia's board as a private equity manager, working closely with the company for years until it was publicly listed on the stock exchange in 2015.

Tuninvest's third fund succeeded in raising some € 150 million, and is similarly fully deployed today. In all three funds, FMO and other development banks were the cornerstone investors, as it remained difficult to find commercial investors to step in.

The next step was to start a pan-African private equity fund. Following preparatory discussions with FMO, the AfricInvest Group was founded, which is active in Anglophone West Africa (with an office in Nigeria), Francophone West and Central Africa (with an office in Cote d'Ivoire), and East and Southern Africa (with an office in Kenya). In 2015, AfricInvest Fund III raised over € 230 million.

While AfricInvest has been active for over 20 years now, the industry around the firm has quickly built traction. Private equity funds have sprung up in many African countries. From an early stage, FMO recognised the need for them to band together. While the field now had scale, there was still a need to make it visible. In 2000, AfricInvest and FMO jointly organised an annual conference on private equity in Africa in order to facilitate the exchange of ideas, inspire collaboration, and attract commercial investors from outside the region. From one of these conferences, the idea emerged of jointly founding an official organisation, the African Private Equity and Venture Capital Association (AVCA), the first of its kind that has established standards in order to attract investors.

Years ago, FMO was the first development bank to step in and help AfricInvest, and now the firm manages a total of around US $1 billion across 14 funds and is invested in 130 companies across 25 African countries. Not bad for a few entrepreneurs that started without a private equity background!

Together with other development banks, FMO had stepped in at the right time. In sixteen years, the private equity market in Africa has gone from being inconsequential to becoming a professional, diverse, continental community. We had helped to open this new and exciting industry to new commercial streams of finance.

CONCLUSION

In this chapter I aimed to showcase the strength, expertise, and value of development finance institutions. Their extensive experience in the private sector in developing countries remains unique, as does their knowledge and long-term view of implementing international standards. These institutions have gone through growing pains in order to mature, making them ideal partners for governments searching to maximise the impact of their increasingly scarce ODA funds. With one euro of ODA money, blended finance can mobilise more than 10 or 20 times the value of that investment to create an impact – an investment that directly contributes to achieving the SDGs.

DFIs have considerable experience in creating blended vehicles or blended structures. In the process, they have earned the confidence of the private sector and have shown that they understand the needs and requirements of commercial investors.

The examples I have mentioned were all concentrated efforts by more than one DFI. While one or two institutions may have been the leading partner, these cases underline the impact such collaborative efforts can have on an entire sector or region. DFIs have demonstrated that the impact this creates goes far beyond that of a single project.

NEW BUSINESS MODELS FOR SUSTAINABLE DEVELOPMENT

In the previous chapter, I demonstrated how development banks can play a crucial role in upscaling new business models. In order to accelerate the implementation of the Global Goals, development banks must now also contribute to the creation of new business models. It is clear that a huge collaborative and financial effort is needed to build and finance new business models where they are most needed: in infrastructure, renewable energy, biodiversity, and inclusive business. It is in these areas that there is a need to develop projects and models that are more effective and yet still bankable. The problem today is not a lack of money but the lack of sustainable development projects.

> *There will always be new and emerging sectors which will need the spark of an institution that can take more risk than others.*
>
> – Aziz Mebarek, founding partner of AfricInvest

THE FUTURE OF SUSTAINABLE FINANCE

In leading up to this point, I have described the paradigm shift towards the Global Goals, examined what business can and must contribute to these goals, and highlighted what the financial sector can do in turn. I have stressed the pivotal and growing role of development finance institutions in meeting the SDGs. Governments should strengthen their international and national development banks so as to optimise the use of government money in reaching the Global Goals while at the same time actively involving businesses, investors, and other relevant parties.

Of course, business and finance can only play a supportive role in reaching the Global Goals if they meet the criteria we have formulated in chapters two and three. It is crucial to start with a profitable business case.

SHARING RISK

Investments currently represent about 20% of global GDP, or roughly US $20 trillion. We need to redirect around 10% of that, or roughly US $2 trillion, towards achieving the Global Goals. That is about the same amount as the yearly annual growth in global GDP. So although the absolute amount appears mind-boggling, it is important to put this into perspective. This is doable. The obstacles to this change in my view are the lack of a sense of urgency in business and governments alike; the dearth of investable/bankable projects; the paucity of incentives; and the lack of sufficient funding in the right places. The money is available – we just need to channel it properly and to redirect it towards sustainable development.

Often when the conversation is about sustainable investments worldwide or inclusive innovative business models, I hear people say that banks and pension funds must be prepared to take on more risks. But is that really what we want? We have seen what can happen when banks start taking higher risks: the most recent example is the risks that banks took with mortgage-backed securities in the 2008 financial crisis. This cost taxpayers a lot of money and ruined many lives as people saw their savings go up in smoke. Financial crises (in other words: too much risk-taking) remain a constant threat the world over. We do not want banks to lose money by taking higher risks because these losses are borne by us as taxpayers. The same goes for our pension money: people do not want to lose their pensions as a result of pension funds having invested in numerous innovative (but risky) sustainable ideas.

What I would like to see is banks and pension funds becoming more open to looking at how they can finance investments and share risks with other parties. We see that most financial institutions get lost in all the new rules and regulations that are continuously being issued; as a result, they do not take the time to develop sustainable strategies that are adapted to their risk models. We need to channel money to those areas where investment can contribute to a better world and then distribute the risk to those who can bear it. This requires collaboration and co-creation: put investors, policymakers, regulators, and risk-takers such as governments and development banks all in one room and give them the chance to co-create solutions. Risk should be clear, simple, and transparent so that financial institutions avoid making the same mistakes they made in the 2008 financial crisis.

The areas that sustainable development must focus on if we are to meet the Global Goals are: infrastructure (roads, ports, telecommunications, etc.), environmental innovations, inclusive business, and expanding the infrastructure of social services. We need to design new business models that are bankable and scalable, especially business models that target those at the base of the economic pyramid. At present, the only such business model of significance is microfinance.

INFRASTRUCTURE FINANCE

FMO developed an innovative project development approach whereby high-impact infrastructure projects with unique Dutch content are developed for emerging markets and developing economies. This approach is called Flying Swans.

Flying Swans
The first Flying Swans programme is to be in Ethiopia and Djibouti, where a FMO-led Dutch business consortium will jointly develop infrastructure projects with a positive impact on food security and agri-logistics. What makes this approach so unique is that the consortium members are the ones that will organise capacity and the financing for early stage development – in other words, project development now has an integrated solution. While project developers traditionally help with, say, the construction and financing of a stand-alone port and leave the port authority with the task of searching for other contractors for

a warehouse and transportation infrastructure, the Flying Swans approach means that companies are already identified to handle the finance and development of the port and a railway and a warehouse. When pitched to me a few years ago, this vision was still developing – it was unclear as to what exactly the initiators wanted, how they planned to do it, and how it would fit into FMO's strategy. But underneath the passion with which the initiators explained their plan, I could sense that this had the potential to be interesting for FMO in the long run.

China, Korea, and Japan already approach infrastructure projects with an integrated solution, pre-aligning the companies needed, the government, the finance, the manpower, and the trade flows. This is what the Netherlands should be doing as well. The Dutch market is filled with high-calibre companies with international ambitions that are geared towards sustainability, and yet these companies are sometimes outpaced by foreign consortia that offer a fully integrated project solution. The Flying Swans would enable Dutch enterprises and investors to offer developing economies integrated solutions to food security problems and climate mitigation.

I organised a roundtable to see if this idea to create the Flying Swans could be of some value. At the roundtable were VNO NCW (the Dutch employer's federation), the Ministry of Infrastructure & Development, the Ministry of Foreign Affairs,, Boskalis (the leading dredging and marine expert), Frugi Venta (the Dutch fruit and vegetables trade association), Mercator Novus (a Dutch strategic consultancy firm), and the Port of Rotterdam. By bringing these parties together, we had identified the key players in project development and introduced them to each other before the project ideas were even on paper.

As development finance institutions grow, governments are increasingly asking them to do more for their home markets while investing in developing countries. Flying Swans does just that by creating a sustainable role for Dutch businesses in trade and simultaneously connecting emerging markets to global value chains. By enabling both the Dutch economy and developing economies to become more robust, we are creating a win-win situation.

Ethiopia quickly signed on to have a cooling logistics system built for the Addis-Djibouti railway. Cooling facilities will be needed to boost Ethiopian exports of perishables and to increase their competitiveness on international markets. This offers new opportunities for Dutch horticultural companies to invest in Ethiopia and increase their exports. South Africa has also signed on to have an unbroken chain of cold storage and distribution facilities for agricultural products built from rural areas to the port in Durban. These are partnerships that I am convinced we will see more of.

FINANCING ENVIRONMENTAL INNOVATIONS

What are the challenges we face in accelerating the scale of investments that address climate change? Here I am referring to wind, solar, geothermal, hydropower, and bio-based projects. The technology is clearly there. The price of generating these kinds of renewable energy is declining as we speak and becoming more competitive with fossil fuels. While renewable energy sources have at times been reliant on subsidies, in many countries where governments invite companies to tender and bid on prices, these subsidies are dropping at an amazing speed. Sustainable energy can therefore compete with fossil fuels in an increasing number of countries. Technologies that are the first of their kind are, however, high risk for financiers and therefore should be backed by government support.

One challenge confronting renewable energy is the fact that they are generated above ground, in contrast to fossil fuels which come exclusively from below the earth's surface. The visual pollution that this causes has sparked protests from communities where sustainable energy sources are being developed in their vicinity. The term NIMBY or "not in my backyard" is becoming commonplace. Hydropower projects can be a particularly delicate issue when it comes to land rights – even more so when indigenous groups are affected. It is important for developers, financiers, and local communities collaborate in order to reach the best possible solution. Project development itself, as well as the number of bankable projects, provide two additional bottlenecks. The process can be too slow, and there is simply a general dearth of bankable projects. We need to speed up project development in combination with finance. Financing energy efficiency is generally lower risk and is a relatively easy case to make as a bankable business. Here, the main issue is one of raising awareness.

Below, I highlight several projects that are in their infancy stage but have the potential to finance sustainable development on a sufficiently large scale. The first case that I describe – the Climate Investor One Fund – is a good example of a structure that accelerates project development and uses blended finance to attract commercial capital, with the development bank serving as a bridge to connect the public and private sectors.

Financing Climate-Change-Related Projects

Imagine you are an entrepreneur and you want to build a wind farm somewhere in Africa. Observing a constant wind each day, you take measurements to give your project idea a valid basis. How do you then transform your idea into reality? Construction is expensive and you will need money that you will probably have to collect from different sources because there are few financiers willing to take on the risk of the full sum. Two years later, you are still trying to raise capital. By then, the loans have become more expensive, you have lost precious time, and the financial viability of the project is dropping. This remains a common story in development.

Climate Investor One

It was clear that we had to find a way to step in earlier to help develop energy projects from the beginning of the process. The solution that FMO came up with is Climate Investor One, a new approach to funding infrastructure projects by which the environmental impact, economic returns, and operating infrastructure can be delivered in a much faster and simpler manner. The facility is unique in the way it combines three investment funds into one facility to finance renewable energy projects at specific stages of the project lifecycle: the development stage, the construction stage, and the operational stage.

Climate Investor One will have significant positive social impact, as the majority of the funding will be invested in the poorest countries. The fund expects to reach six million underserved people and support 23,000 direct and 300,000 indirect jobs. Further, Climate Investor One aims to achieve an estimated annual avoidance of 1.5 million tons in carbon dioxide emissions – the equivalent of 500,000 cars off the roads each year.

Climate Investor One was the result of a challenge I presented to our energy department at FMO. The Global Innovation Lab for Climate Finance was holding a contest in which the best climate-change-related projects in the private sector would receive endorsements in their fundraising activities. Our energy department enthusiastically took on the challenge, working day and night for two years to pursue a side project, bringing in Phoenix InfraWorks – an equally enthusiastic and professional private equity fund – to help. All their hard work paid off as they were selected as one of four prize-winning projects! Climate Investor One has received firm expressions of interest from the Dutch, UK, and US governments as well as an English pension fund and a Danish export financier. The prize was awarded in 2015 and Climate Investor One is expected to start execution this year.

If we are to shift toward a sustainable future in time, we need to streamline the sustainable development process. Climate Investor One represents an important step in the right direction.

Financing Off-Grid Energy Solutions

Emerging markets need new business models, especially in the area of off-grid energy solutions for rural areas. The distances between people in many countries make the cost of transportation and construction of electrical infrastructure prohibitively high. Off-grid energy solutions would bypass these costs. The basic business logic is there. Solar is cheaper and healthier than kerosene, and you only need a single device. This makes it an ideal solution that can be catered to those at the base of the economic pyramid. Though I have yet to see any large-scale solutions, I know that there is considerable experimentation going on in various countries. The same is true for clean cookstoves that are either more efficient or that avoid using wood altogether, which also addresses a major health risk. While there have been attempts to make off-grid energy solutions available, we are still searching for scalable business models. In such cases, seed money can make the difference.

ElectriFI

Development finance institutions could play a key role in stimulating and supporting the development of off-grid energy solutions at scale. With this in mind, the European Commission recently approached me as chair of the association of European Development Finance Institutions (EDFI) with the idea of setting up a fund dedicated to off-grid rural electrification projects. The Commission had € 75 million for European development banks to manage and invest, and it wanted to find a way to provide access to energy while tapping into the huge potential of the many new, innovative models that could bring reliable, clean, and affordable energy to the many who lack access to reliable energy. FMO was asked to develop a financing mechanism to support private sector initiatives in sustainable energy. With our technical assistance, a bankable solution was devised which came to be called Electrification Financing Initiative, or ElectriFI.

ElectriFI is a perfect example of blended finance: each European development bank can make use of the fund to finance projects that meet the requirements. The initiative focuses on collaboration with other financiers rather than competition, with European DFIs seeking to fill any gaps in funding for smaller private sector projects and to be additional in all cases. ElectriFI can be used by European development banks to provide both technical assistance and risk capital for rural off-grid electrification projects. With a winning model in place, the EU is currently in the process of designing an Agriculture Financing Initiative (AgriFI) and is looking into creating similar funds in the areas of education, health care, and forestry.

> *Doing the riskiest projects and still finding a way to make money – now that is truly sustainable. That is a compliment to your ability, your expertise.*
>
> – Maurits Groen, Founder WakaWaka, Netherlands

The Story of Waka Waka

With a US $48,000 Kickstarter crowdfunding campaign, Maurits Groen co-founded WakaWaka in 2012 to deliver a high-quality, off-grid power solution to people in Africa. There are over one billion people worldwide without access to energy. The problem is particularly acute in Africa, where the sheer distances between villages provide a serious challenge to energy distribution in terms of the costs and resources involved. The main form of lighting currently being used in Africa is the kerosene lamp, which is damaging to both its users and the environment. Indoor pollution resulting from the kerosene and inefficient stoves kills more people every year than AIDS and Malaria combined. The sun is a free source of energy – and even better, it's evenly distributed. WakaWaka recognised the huge impact that solar-powered lights could bring to rural communities.

The WakaWaka Light is both the most efficient and longest-lasting solar-powered flashlight in the world, with a charge lifetime of 80 hours. The WakaWaka Power doubles as a flashlight and a telephone charger. While WakaWaka sells these products in developed markets with a 'buy one, give one' policy, meaning one lamp is donated to an emergency relief fund with every purchase, the cost that comes with quality remains an issue in the developing markets where they are most needed. The one-time investment can easily cost a family two months' worth of the local average salary of US $25. To work around this problem, WakaWaka developed a pilot for the Virtual Grid – the world's first telecom-based personal solar pay-as-you-go system. In this way, people could own a WakaWaka flashlight for no more than a few dollars and thereby overcome the high upfront investment. By buying a scratch card with a code to be texted to WakaWaka, customers would receive a unique activation code based on the week. With one dollar, a family had access to power for a week.

Safe, clean energy could now provide the light by which children study and recharge phones needed for business, thus generating a positive impact on family health, education, and economic opportunities. Even with these benefits, finding investment capital was difficult. This was brand-new territory and therefore high-risk; moreover, at € 1.5 million it was too small of a sum for a traditional direct investment by a development bank. Recognising the tremendous impact potential, FMO invested € 600,000 – roughly one-third of the total required capital – in the project alongside WakaWaka and a private investor. Together, we launched the pilot in Rwanda in three rural districts in 2014. From there, the model can become scalable over time.

Financing Forestry Projects

Our forests are in decline on a global scale. Between logging for wood products, clearing land for farming, and fires both natural and accidental, the planet's lungs have shrunk by 0.2% per year since the 1990s. In the meantime, the world's carbon emissions have been steadily increasing. But the trend can be reversed, and forests will have to play a key role in that reversal. An investment of one dollar in reforestation or protecting a hectare forest reduces ten to twenty times more greenhouse gases than one dollar invested in renewable energy.

Forestry funds manage and develop forestry projects spread throughout the world, working with different species, soils, altitudes, climates, and communities. An investor in forest equity not only earns a profit of between 8-15% but also benefits from a myriad of positive impacts that forests can bring. Aside from helping reduce the amount of carbon dioxide in the atmosphere, forestry projects create stable, sustainable employment for the many unskilled workers needed in the continuous cycle of planting, cutting, and replanting. Of course, all such projects face risks – political risks, the risk of fires, or uncertainty of obtaining community approval of the project. But just as in any business, managing the process is the key to success. The local community can either be the match that destroys a foreign project or the water that saves the livelihood they helped to build. Forestry projects are therefore dependent on broad community support.

The first harvest cycle of a forestry project can take anywhere between seven and 25 years based on the species of tree. To be made into an electricity pole, a eucalyptus tree needs about eight years to grow, while a teak tree whose wood becomes denser and darker with age can take up to 25 years before it is ready to be made into luxurious furniture. In order to bridge the 5-10 year gap until the first harvest can be sold, investors with a long-term horizon are needed. The obvious candidate would be development banks, but if such forestry projects are to be scaled up, they will need the help of climate funds, family offices, governments, and commercial long-term investors such as pension funds. This is where blended finance comes in.

FMO invests in a number of international forestry funds, and we also invest directly in two forestry companies in East Africa. Our forestry investments now represent €80-90 million or 1% of our total balance sheet. While this is a start, I firmly believe that FMO should be doing more. We are now in discussions with the European Union to draw in finance for a collaboration between FMO, DEG, FinnFund, and the seven largest forestry companies.

Aside from being resistant to fluctuations in the economy, wood is a product in high demand and will be for years to come. If we hope to continue harvesting wood, we must begin doing so in a way that increases the earth's capacity to remove carbon dioxide instead of reducing it. Sustainable forestry generates profits as well as rural employment.

This needs to become a global focus and an area that more financial institutions and governments step into. The next step that needs to be taken is to find a financial model for landscape restoration, which would recover degraded lands and make them productive and sustainable again. The urgent challenge now is to develop bankable solutions in this area.

Althelia Climate Fund

The Althelia Climate Fund, which was developed with the support of Conservation International (CI), finances sustainable land-use projects and enterprise-based conservation of nature and its resources. The fund aims to invest US $150 million in Africa and Latin America in sustainable agriculture, certified commodities, and environmental services. Althelia's projects typically have multiple revenue streams. Revenues from forest conservation in the form of carbon credits is usually one of them. Such credits are referred to as REDD+, which stands for "reducing emissions from deforestation in developing countries", a mechanism that is being considered by the UN Framework Convention on Climate Change. Althelia aims to demonstrate that financial performance can be fully aligned with sound environmental stewardship and social development. Four Dutch companies – Desso, Eneco, Essent, and FMO – agreed to buy part of the REDD+ carbon credits from Althelia.

One of the investments of the funds is an innovative public-private partnership in which the Peruvian state preserves more than 1.3 million hectares of pristine mountain rainforest within the Cordillera Azul National Park, supporting the sustainable land use of its rich buffer zone of 2.5 million hectares. The park is located in San Martin, one of the largest protected areas in Peru, and is home to around 6,000 plant species, more than 80 large and medium-size mammals, around 180 species of fish, and over 600 species of birds.

The project will protect this unique biodiversity and restore degraded lands with agroforestry systems (cocoa & coffee) in the buffer zone so as to improve the livelihood of small farmers and local communities. As a consequence, it will avoid more than 15 million tonnes of CO_2 emissions over the next six years due to the reduction of deforestation. This reduction in emissions is equivalent to all the flights that will pass through London's Heathrow Airport over the same period.

FMO and the European Investment Bank have each invested US $15 million in the fund, allowing it to close its first round of financing and subsequently attract *follow-up funding from other development finance institutions and commercial investors.*

INCLUSIVE FINANCE

According to the World Bank, some 2.5 billion people around the world do not have a formal bank account. This lack of access to professional financial services is a significant impediment to poverty reduction. Increasing financial inclusion would thus help to alleviate poverty but also reduce income inequality and even contribute to economic growth. This is why financial inclusion is incorporated as a target in the UN's first Sustainable Development Goal of ending poverty.

The benefits of financial inclusion to individual citizens and to society as a whole are self-evident: inclusive finance can accelerate the process of providing better access to – and increasing the calibre of – basic social services such as education, health care, sanitation, and drinking water. Although ensuring that all its citizens have access to basic financial services should be the responsibility of the government, many developing economies lack the resources to address inclusion.

Efforts to increase financial inclusion have been given a boost in recent years by new technologies such as the internet and smartphones, which make it cheaper to deliver financial services. Just consider the extra time, energy, and resources one needs to expend in order to get access to basic healthcare services when the closest hospital is thirty miles away. In bringing down transaction and delivery costs, technology can be the breakthrough needed to finance sustainable development. The best example of inclusive finance is microfinance, which provides access to credit for those at the bottom of the pyramid.

The Gender Finance Gap

An overwhelming majority of the world's poorest people are women. At the base of the economic pyramid – those that make under US $8 per day – women are largely unbanked and financially illiterate. In the markets in which development banks work, women often have less access to finance than men. In many countries, if a woman wanted to set up a business and needed finance, she faces more obstacles than men. How can a woman provide collateral for a loan when the law prevents her from owning land?

Funding Female Entrepreneurs

Sustainable development aims to close the gender gap by including more women in the financial system. This is an area that FMO aims to focus on. Although providing the funds for banks to extend loans to women is important, what FMO offers that has even more value is technical assistance. By educating banks and thinking together with local parties as well as raising awareness about their product structuring and service delivery, FMO is able to steer clients towards offering products and services that tailor to women's means – products that, for example, use a cash flow analysis rather than collateral to assess investment risk. As women in developing economies often lack financial role models, FMO is active in creating networks to connect, educate, and assist women to address their technical needs.

Alongside IFC and the Goldman Sachs Foundation, FMO is investing US $30 million in the Women's Entrepreneur Debt Fund, which aims to raise US $600 million in total. This money will be channeled to financial institutions in emerging markets and developing economies to fund female entrepreneurs.

In addition to striving to close the gender finance gap, businesses should look further and address women's barriers to positions of power. Women are often underrepresented in leadership positions – a problem that spreads far beyond the developing world. Promoting and facilitating a company culture that upholds gender equality makes business sense. FMO now focuses on gender diversity at the management level as part of our due diligence because we are convinced that including women in leadership positions enriches decision-making with valuable perspectives that would otherwise be excluded. At the end of the day, better decisions translate into better profitability.

Financing Small Farmers

Farmer finance is another form of inclusive finance. The challenge here is how to reach small farmers and provide them with access to finance and the means to improve their productivity. Smallholder farmers have particular needs that differ from other entrepreneurs due to the volatility of their output and the risks they shoulder – in particular the risks posed by variable weather patterns. Many end up falling between two stools, as they are too small to be considered by commercial banks but too big to be eligible for microcredit.

The Smallholder Finance Facility

FMO is currently collaborating with the Sustainable Trade Initiative (IDH), a Dutch NGO that works with small farmers around the world, to provide financing for smallholder farmers throughout the value chain. I met the executive director of IDH, over lunch in 2013, and I recall how we expressed our mutual surprise as to why we had never worked together before. Our organisations were both private-public partnerships that were focused on building sustainable supply chains. It was a natural fit, and we jumped at the chance to work together.

The cooperation, however, did not proceed as smoothly as we had expected. Within eighteen months, the situation had reached a low point and we were ready to go our separate ways. What had gone wrong? When we came together to assess the situation, we realised that our two organisations came from different worlds and that we were having difficulty understanding one another. Instead of focusing on our differences, however, we had to understand one another clearly and identify where we could complement each other. IDH had the local knowledge of the farmers that came with years of intimate experience in the local community: it knew who we could trust, whether or not the cacao farm was using child labour, or whether the produce was organic as the customer expected. FMO needed this information to assess the risk and set up the financing. By combining our strengths, we were eventually able to create yet another promising model for inclusive finance. This involved setting up a specialised team with its own investment committee composed of two IDH colleagues and two of our own – the first mixed team of its kind.

The Smallholder Finance Facility is a good example of blended finance where the grant money of an NGO is combined with the risk capital of a DFI and where we mobilise pre-financing by buyers in the value chain before the harvest. Because of the informal, varied nature of inclusive finance around the world, it is difficult to say whether this model can be used elsewhere, but I do believe that forging new partnerships is an essential means to achieving financial inclusion. In addition, the development of financial technologies such as mobile banking will be key in bringing financial services to an increasing number of people by substantially lowering transaction costs.

MASSIF, The Inclusive Fund

Set to be launched in 2016, MASSIF 2.0 is a Dutch government fund of € 500 million managed by FMO that is dedicated exclusively to increasing financial inclusion by providing equity to microfinance institutions and rural SMEs. It is a fund whose roots reach back as far as my own within FMO, where it started in 1988 as the Small Enterprise Fund. The innovation at that time was to provide local currency loans to financial institutions whose clients were medium, small, and micro entrepreneurs. Within ten years, the Small Enterprise Fund had provided more than one million micro-entrepreneurs access to credit, translating into more than € 1.4 billion. It was a unique fund in those days that built up a portfolio of about € 300 million over almost 20 years with contributions from the Dutch state. The MASSIF Fund was created by merging the portfolios of the SME Fund, the Balkan Fund (which financed SMEs in the Balkans after the war), and the Seed Capital Fund (which financed start-up financial institutions and private equity funds).

MASSIF 2.0 targets those at the base of the economic pyramid, servicing entrepreneurs without access to finance, with a special focus on female entrepreneurs, young entrepreneurs, small farmers, rural SMEs, and new business models. The fund will start with a portfolio of almost € 500 million, which should allow it to generate a substantial impact. In a field that has lacked scale until now, it is important for DFIs such as FMO to channel funding into supporting new and innovative service delivery models.

Arise, A New Approach to Investing in the Financial Sector in Africa

While international banks are reducing their activities in Africa, because of regulatory or other risk- related reasons, one commercial and two development banks show that they believe in the future of Africa. Mid 2016, Rabobank, Norfund and FMO decided to create a unique partnership, called Arise, an investment platform for further development of the financial sector in Africa.

This new entity, Arise, will take and manage strategic minority stakes in financial institutions in Sub Sahara Africa. The goal is to help develop these local institutions into strong, and stable organizations thus increasing access to finance. Arise will offer technical assistance programs, as well as supporting the investee companies financially as a shareholder. Doing so, Arise will empower African banks to expand and improve services to their clients.

Arise will have an explicit long term sustainable development strategy. The planned structure of Arise will provide more muscle for new investments and room to employ in-house experts in areas such as risk, credit, sustainability, technology, etc. Furthermore, Arise will support local banks thereby strengthening their capital base and reduce the likelihood of local banks either going under (as recently happened in Kenya) or being taken over by international banking groups. There is clear value for any country to have strong local banks in terms of local market focus as well as job creation.

Arise will really be able to create impact, because of the scale on which it will operate. Arise has at its inception a portfolio in over 20 countries, and US $660 million invested in financial institutions. The goal is to grow these investments to US $1 billion. The key ambition is to build strong and stable local banks that will serve retail, small and medium enterprises, the rural sector, and clients who have not previously had access to financial services.

Arise is a new kind of vehicle that takes a very long term view, much longer than traditional private equity funds. Such a long term vision is crucial to invest in the financial sector, as it takes between 10 and 20 years to build a strong, stable and sustainable financial sector. Such vehicles with a long term investment horizon can be an example for other sectors like renewable energy and forestry.

FINANCING SOCIAL SERVICES

Financing Healthcare

Most governments in Africa do not or cannot provide adequate health services for their population. This has to do with a lack of institutional capacity as well as a lack of resources. The private sector can mobilise both the capacity and the resources to effectively deliver health services. However, sustainable and profitable healthcare business models are hard to come by. Luckily, there are always pioneers.

The Investment Fund for Health in Africa

Here I want to highlight the Investment Fund for Health in Africa (IFHA), which began in 2007. The initiative behind IFHA came from the PharmAccess Foundation, an organisation whose aim is to contribute to building sustainable healthcare in Africa. The institute was founded by Joep Lange, an extraordinary and inspiring man who was at the forefront in the fight against HIV/AIDS as well as many other initiatives to improve healthcare access for poor communities in Africa. I had the privilege of serving on the board of the Tuberculosis Foundation in the Netherlands together with Joep Lange.

IFHA is a private equity fund that invests in private healthcare, in small and medium-sized hospitals and clinics, and in health insurance as well as in the manufacturing and distribution of healthcare products throughout the continent. Based on the experience and the success of its first fund in 2016, IFHA recently began raising a second fund with a target of US $135 million. IFHA is the first private equity fund in Africa to build a profitable portfolio in healthcare. It has invested in Nigeria, Tanzania, and Uganda, reached out to roughly 800,000 patients, and provided insurance for about 700,000 people. IFHA is leading the way, and it is now key to prove that the model is scalable. IFHA is financed by development banks including FMO, IFC, and other impact investors.

PharmAccess Group started the Medical Credit Fund (MCF) in 2009 to support private healthcare facilities in Africa. These facilities are located in urban and rural areas where they are run by medical practitioners and provide basic primary healthcare to local low-income communities. Most patients visit the clinic for common illnesses such as malaria, HIV/AIDS, and respiratory infections. MCF has taken a big step by providing guarantees to the local banks that channel credit to their clients. MCF operates in four countries and has provided services to almost 1,500 clinics, which translates to more than 600,000 patient visits a month.

IFHA and MCF have shown that business models in healthcare in Africa can be successful, that they can have a significant positive impact on low-income communities, and that they can be financially sustainable. Both initiatives are financed by development banks such as FMO, IFC, and the African Development Bank as well as government agencies.

Financing Education

A recent Unesco report highlighted the poor quality of education in most developing countries, revealing that half of the youth in South Asia and one-third of those in Africa who have completed four years of schooling cannot read properly. The failure of governments to deliver a decent education and to increase teacher incomes in Africa has led to a boom in private education. The World Bank estimates that one-fifth of the primary school pupils in Africa are enrolled in private schools, most of which are single operators. This only widens the gap between the privileged and the disadvantaged in developing countries, where income inequality is already at deplorable levels.

Bridge International Academies

It is time to turn the tide. Through its investment in Novastar, an African private equity fund supporting exceptional entrepreneurs in East Africa, FMO is indirectly invested in Bridge International Academies. Based in Kenya but rapidly expanding into the rest of Africa and soon Asia, Bridge is the world's largest for-profit chain of nursery and primary schools, offering affordable high-quality primary education for low-income families. Using technology and data, Bridge achieves enormous efficiencies both in terms of the overhead costs required to run a school and in terms of raising the quality of the education. The company's goal is to educate 10 million children across a dozen countries by 2025. Bridge receives financing from the Novastar fund in addition to development banks such as IFC, CDC, and foundations such as the Bill and Melinda Gates Foundation and the Chan Zuckerberg Initiative.

Innova Schools

In Peru, a country that I know well, the education system currently lags far behind countries with a similar average income. Indeed, the Inter-American Development Bank recently noted that raising the quality of its education system was one of biggest challenges Peru faced. This need is all the more pressing due to the burgeoning demand for good quality education from a rapidly growing middle class. Between 2003 and 2009, more than one million families joined the middle class, and although many of these households are willing to spend up to 20% of their household income on education, there are simply not enough schools in the country that combine quality and affordability.

One successful businessman, Carlos Rodriguez Pastor, decided to do something about this. He created a chain of affordable private schools called Innova Schools that rely on blended learning, a form of education that uses technology and guided independent study, to stimulate kids to be creative, flexible, and critical. The cost per child is US $130 per month – far cheaper than most private schools – and the schools' results in reading and math are far better than both the public and private schools in Peru. Innova Schools' profitable and innovative business model was partly financed by the Inter-American Development Bank.

CONCLUSION

I wanted to demonstrate in this chapter that partnerships are essential to creating new and effective business models that will allow the global community to reach the Global Goals by 2030. There are already many promising examples in various sectors upon which future collaborations can build. To my mind, these initiatives begin with the entrepreneur – the person with the business idea and the risk capital to create a new model. The entrepreneur needs support in creating the business model and then implementing and financing it. These partners can be either other businesses or NGOs working on different points of the supply chain or in the target communities at the bottom of the pyramid. For financing, a project starts with a development bank, government, or other impact investor willing to step in and share the risk with the entrepreneur.

I selected a number of nascent business models that have the potential to scale up in size as well as in their impact on low-income communities and the environment. This is one important way to go forward. We need more innovative partnerships to contribute solutions to our global challenges. When partnered with entrepreneurs, national and international development banks can be the key to creating bankable business models and organising the financing needed for sustainable development.

FMO'S TRANSITION TO SUSTAINABLE DEVELOPMENT

So far I have covered the global movement towards sustainable development and the role of development banks therein. But what does a company's transition towards sustainability look like in practice? In this final chapter I want to offer some insights into how FMO has navigated and adapted to the shifting global landscape during my time as CEO. The strategic changes were based on FMO's strength and intended to strengthen FMO even further in the light of our shareholders wishes' and the global changes described in chapter two. As I noted in chapter three, we wanted to place FMO in a position that would better allow it to support companies in making sustainability central to their mission, so as to raise the investment needed to reach the Global Goals. FMO would need to be an adequate partner for other players in the impact investing space in order to scale the investments for sustainable development as well as develop and finance the new business models described in previous chapters.

OUR CULTURE: PRAGMATIC AND PROBLEM-SOLVING

When I started as CEO in 2008, the main question I confronted was what the strategy should be for the coming years. In the decades leading up to that point, FMO had been successful: we had grown at a pace of about 10% per year, we had been profitable, and we had generated development impact. In 2005, FMO had stopped receiving injections from the Dutch state to strengthen its risk capital and now stood on its own feet. In 2008, FMO received its banking licence, placing itself under a clear and consistent supervision framework. This made us more attractive as a shareholder of financial institutions in our markets. Our relationship with our main shareholder, the Dutch state, was good. FMO was recognised by its clients and partners as a pragmatic, problem-solving DFI.

These are strange folk. They're not driven by money. It's moral conviction. That's very refreshing.

– Connor McEnroy, Chairman Sudameris Bank, Paraguay

FMO has always had a strong culture. As a mission-driven organisation, FMO employees are passionate in pursuing the greater good. The new generation is increasingly future-conscious, and this also helps us attract the best talent. Because they have chosen to work for a development bank rather than our more lucrative commercial cousins, our co-workers are intrinsically motivated by the desire to have an impact on society. With that as our starting point, we began designing FMO's new strategy just before the outbreak of the financial crisis in 2008. It was a time in which there was a significant amount of capital flowing into emerging markets as well as investors looking for new market opportunities and taking on more risk.

FMO'S NEW STRATEGY: MAKING CHOICES

A jack-of-all-trades is the master of none. FMO is a small institution in a big world, and in order to add value I knew that our activities needed more focus. I felt that we had to shape the new strategy using the knowledge and experience of everybody, so we held World Cafe sessions in which more than half of the FMO staff took part. The message coming out of those sessions was that FMO had to add more value and that we should focus more on poorer countries. Our employees also felt we should focus on sectors and on sustainability and that we should catalyse more. But most importantly, we identified what areas we were no longer going to cover. It was the first time we had done this at FMO. We chose to focus 80% of our activities on only three sectors – the financial sector, energy, and housing – and to shift the organisation from a regional to a sectoral focus in order to strengthen our knowledge and network specifically within these three sectors. And in order to concentrate on low-income countries, we decided to stop doing business in four of the larger and richer countries: Russia, Brazil, Kazakhstan, and Mexico.

By providing access to our expertise and network, we could increase the added value we offered our clients and in that way achieve our ambition of becoming the industry leader in the area of sustainability. The supervisory board approved our new strategy just as the financial crisis began to unfold.

THE FINANCIAL CRISIS

Having signed for the position on the first of October, 2008, two weeks after the fall of the Lehman Brothers, I stepped into a financial world that appeared to be crumbling beneath our feet. People were in a state of panicked shock, dreading that the worst was yet to come. Who would fall next? FMO had suffered the biggest loss in its history in the final quarter of 2008, just after I started as CEO. But while we had suffered a very big loss in the initial shock, FMO still realised a profit over the whole year.

The financial crisis of 2008 was a turning point in the history of the financial sector in that it gave our business model more validation. We hadn't invested in speculation; instead, we had invested in the real economy. We had aimed for a consistent 6% return – something almost laughable before the crisis – and suddenly we found people curious as to how we were still making it. The crisis hadn't devastated the emerging markets and developing economies – indeed, that was where the future of economic growth was. It was a moment for FMO's self esteem to grow. Suddenly a long-term vision based on ethics had gained authority and recognition.

Later that month, I travelled to the World Bank meetings in Washington with the two other members of FMO's management board. What we encountered there was nothing but doom and gloom everywhere we turned. This naturally led to serious discussions on whether we should go ahead and implement our new strategy, which would be the biggest reorganisation in FMO's history, in the middle of this crisis. In the end, we decided that we needed to be bold and move forward. All three of us were convinced that the changes we had chosen would be crucial for the role that FMO had to play in the long run.

WALKING THE WALK

We had defined our ambition to be the industry leader in sustainability. There was much doubt within FMO about whether an organisation as small as ours could become the leader in such a wide field. How were we to define 'leading', anyway? I remember having dinner with three experts in environmental and social standards and putting that question on the table. Their answer was simple: do what you have stated as your ideal – that is, ensure that your clients implement the highest international standards such as the IFC performance standards. By doing that, you will be the leader in sustainability. And that is what we did. We had open and meaningful dialogues with our clients, taking the time to understand what was realistically doable for them given their local circumstances rather than simply ticking boxes. An important step was to give our clients an interest rebate when they met the environmental and social standards agreed upon. That showed our clients that we were really walking the walk. The other key step – one that we had made a year earlier – was to take all our environmental and social specialists and move them from the risk department to the front office, thereby putting them and sustainability at the core of our organisation.

I have found it important to visibly demonstrate my support for the implementation of environmental and social standards with our clients. I have made several business trips focused entirely on the implementation of Environmental and Social Management Systems (ESMS) with our financial institution clients. This helped show them that we mean what we say. Normally my visits where focused on discussing financial results, so the fact that the CEO's visit would focus "merely" on Environmental and

Social (ES) was a genuine eye-opener for our clients. Because of my position, I was able to connect to our clients at the CEO-to-CEO level, the management board to management board level. We would invite the bank's E&S specialists to these meetings, which helped to empower them within their organisation. We hoped to make it clear to them that if the CEO came to discuss these issues, they were of real importance to FMO. And it worked.

In some cases, I encountered a healthy initial resistance. In such cases our meeting succeeded in sparking an internal reflection within the management board on the business value of environmental and social standards. In most cases, these meetings triggered the business-wide implementation of such standards from the top down. Visiting the same banks some years later, we were now at the point/stage of discussing energy efficiency as a business line. That was when I felt a real step had been taken: moving from ESG as a risk management system to identifying the business opportunities therein. This was exactly what I had hoped would happen.

CORRECTING OUR COURSE

After two years, it became clear that FMO should include the agri-food sector as a focus. We should probably have made that decision at the start of the reorganisation, but at that moment I had not dared to because our results in the agri-food sector had been loss making. It was clear, however, that the Dutch government was also starting to focus more on this sector and that FMO had to contribute to a pressing worldwide problem. How else could we help to ensure that, with the same land area and less water use, there would enough food for nine billion people in 2050?
Instead of the agri-food sector, though, we had decided to focus on housing. Three years into our strategy, we evaluated the housing sector results. They were poor. In the face of rapid urbanisation, our predictions that other development banks would join us in this important sector had proven to be wrong. We did not have much of a choice but to stop our activities there despite how crucial this sector was for inclusive development. It was a painful decision, as our housing team had worked passionately to build up this sector portfolio.

OUR SHAREHOLDER

In implementing FMO's strategy, our dialogue and relationship with the government plays a fundamental role. Ultimately, the government is key to FMO's future because it owns more than 90% of FMO's capital. FMO exists because of the political decision to create an organisation that can add value to the government's policies towards the developing world. Without the government's support, FMO could not exist in its actual form. In order to avoid having to change the strategy with each political cycle, it was important for us to try to anticipate the long-term trends in development policy. This was reflected in our decision to focus more on low-income countries, SMEs, and agriculture. In our 2012-2016 strategy And we chose to incorporate green and inclusive growth into our core objectives, as it was an important element of government policy.

What has been key to FMO's success is our strong governance structure combined with the trust we have built up with the Dutch government, which has enabled us to keep daily politics at arm's length as much as possible. Nonetheless, we are facing the growing pressure of becoming a bigger organisation. The amount FMO invests in developing countries will in a few years match or even exceed the government's yearly ODA contributions. As FMO's role continues to grow, the Dutch government has become increasingly involved over the years in our remuneration policies as well as the nominations of members of our supervisory and management boards and the way we handle such issues as human rights in our projects. As a result, we must increase our efforts to demonstrate to the government and to the public the positive impact that FMO is realising through its activities.

THE POWER TO CONVENE

In 2010, on FMO's 40th anniversary, we hosted a conference entitled *The Future of Banking* that gathered together more than 300 bankers, supervisors, and entrepreneurs from over 60 different countries as well as inspirational speakers. We felt it was important for us to add value by opening up our network and knowledge to our clients. Bringing people together gives them the opportunity to share, discuss, and learn from each other. We wanted to use the bank's extensive network to facilitate new connections. Over the years, we have organised some particularly thought-provoking conferences. In the past, speakers have included such figures as Paul Gilding, the ex-CEO of Greenpeace, who shared his view on the limits to our species' growth; Queen Maxima of the Netherlands in her capacity as special advisor to UN Secretary General Ban Ki-moon on financial inclusion; Thomas Sedlacek, former member of the Czech Republic's National Economic Council; and Magnus Lindkvist, an esteemed futurologist. Since then, we have repeated this conference every two years. The feedback from our clients has been very positive: they valued the access they had to FMO's network at the conference and were inspired with new ideas that they could apply in their own institutions.

In 2016, FMO also hosted *Making Solar Bankable*, another 'first of its kind' conference that attracted over 400 international participants to focus on the issue of unlocking capital for new solar project development in emerging markets.

HOSTING MEANINGFUL DIALOGUES

Following the implementation of our new strategy, we came up with the idea of introducing internal discussions which we called 'dilemma dialogues'. These dialogues were a chance for FMO employees to openly discuss their concerns and doubts while sharing tools to disentangle risk issues. With a clear picture of the matter at hand, we can assess our problems and work toward solutions. Dilemma dialogues have also been key in our push to collaborate with other organisations. We engage in them with our clients. At our *Future of Banking* Academy held every other year, we invite our clients to take part in dilemma dialogues to exchange their knowledge and experiences from around the world. We also do this with our stakeholders in order to narrow the gap between our world and theirs. At our 'dilemma dinners', we invite NGOs, government officials, knowledge partners, bankers, and entrepreneurs to the table to take part in an open conversation to address all the hazards involved in financing sustainable development. We find these discussions to be both helpful and increasingly necessary, as they help to create a common language and build mutual trust. By bringing parties together – each voicing their concerns with the intent of reconciling dilemmas – we are learning to understand one another better.

INNOVATION@WORK

After three years of successfully implementing our strategy, it was clear that FMO had to evolve further. The emerging markets were doing well. There was more capital flowing in, which was pushing development banks into new markets so as to remain additional. But I knew that the danger of success lies in becoming too complacent. I talked with some consultants who had trouble grasping my unease. Everything was going well, they said, and you want to change?

I felt we had to create some disorder to shake things up a bit. Marijn came up with the novel idea of inviting an artist, a man who had stepped out of the financial system, to construct a mosaic sculpture in FMO's central hallway in collaboration with our colleagues. That created quite some controversy and commotion – certainly disorder – and challenged our co-workers to reconsider their own assumptions in dealing with someone with a radically different point of view. Perhaps less disruptive but equally effective were the "knowledge coffees" we introduced to get employees to come out of their respective departments and share knowledge and ideas over coffee in a café-like atmosphere in our restaurant. While these may seem like little things, it often only takes a conversation to inspire the next innovation.

We organised a retreat with all the managers and directors of FMO to discuss where FMO was at that moment in time. We came to the conclusion that we were at the end of a cycle and that it was time to work on creating a new perspective to avoid a slow decline. In reaching this conclusion with the entire middle management, we created collective self-awareness and a sense of urgency. After that, each manager and director was asked to make small videos of innovative entrepreneurs who had reinvented their companies. We managed to collect and learn from fascinating examples such as the creation of the cargo bike to transport children, a massive success in the Netherlands, and Desso, a carpet producer with a cradle-to-cradle philosophy.

I was convinced that we needed to innovate in order to remain a frontrunner in our markets and to continue making a difference. The question was: is innovation something you organise in a company or does it arise naturally with the right people? At FMO, innovation has been mostly organic and based on the passion of our investment officers with both new ideas and the perseverance to make them happen. The bank has a healthy culture in which everyone is encouraged to pursue that which they believe in. Over the years I have learned to trust my intuition, especially with regards to the innovative initiatives within FMO. There have been several such initiatives, and at times I supported them out of the simple belief that that was what we had to do. I intrinsically liked these initiatives and intuitively felt they were important. These are the kind of innovative ideas that ultimately drive FMO forward.

To enable innovation and to encourage creative ideas within the organisation, we created the role of innovation officer and an innovation board whose mission is to help these ideas come to life. Admittedly, this is a lot of work. It can often be very frustrating because it is difficult to define concrete outcomes. However, it is ultimately what helps bring out innovative ideas.

BRILLIANT FAILURES

In order to stimulate our employees to take initiatives that risk ending in failure, we introduced the concept of "Brilliant Failures". When in 2011 we decided to stop our activities in housing, I accepted the company-wide award for the most Brilliant Failure on behalf of the housing sector team, to acknowledge and commend their four years of effort and daring. It is in these moments essential to gather people so that we can acknowledge each other, learn together from our mistakes, and foster a culture of trial and error.

On a more personal note, I was quite passionately involved in developing a new entrepreneurial concept meant to transform emerging markets by scaling such green consumer goods as solar lights, cookstoves, and water purification bags for people at the base of the economic pyramid. FMO was to work together with one of most innovative companies in the Netherlands to deliver these products, and I saw it as a fantastic opportunity. However, this idea failed to gain traction within FMO, despite my support, because in the end no one in the company wanted to take on the project. I had forgotten to gauge the organisation's interest in

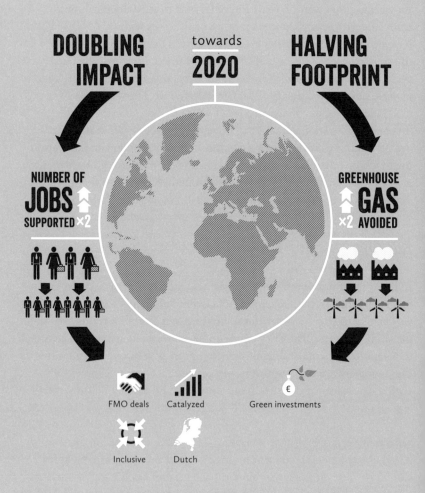

Our strategy has been shaped by our mission to empower entrepreneurs to build a better world.

this project. I had made the mistake of telling the entrepreneur the idea had been approved before checking that all the pieces were actually in place. In the end, this proved to be a very painful yet valuable lesson.

FMO'S LONG-TERM VISION

As I mentioned in chapter two, it was back in 2010 that I was introduced to *Vision 2050*, and I understood right away that setting out this long-term vision could motivate our employees to work for change. The things that we were doing at the time and the choices we were making were very close to the ideas presented in *Vision 2050*. With regards to sectors, we had already chosen the financial sector, energy, agri-food, and forestry – the most crucial sectors in the Vision. We were focusing on governance and transparency as well. This vision made it very clear what needed to be done to enable nine billion people to live well within the limits of our planet.

The outcome of the internal discussions on strategy that took place in 2011 with managers and directors, which was based on *Vision 2050*, was that FMO decided to strive to become the leading impact investor. I was not very happy with this outcome because I did not understand what actions this would actually lead to. We needed to make this objective concrete – something tangible by which we could steer the organisation, a horizon to aim for – and we needed to make our ambition the central focus of our organisation. I therefore opted for a more quantifiable goal: to double our impact and halve our footprint. My colleagues pushed back. How will we achieve that? Will it succeed? There were many unknowns. I didn't know how we were going to develop a strategy based on this goal, but I was ready to figure it out with everyone involved. What I did know was that if the destination was clear, we would find the right solutions.

It was a struggle to choose which indicators to use. Initially, we selected 68 metrics, but it was clear that we were looking for perfection instead of making it doable. Once we realised that making it complex was simple and making it simple was complex, we chose to focus on just two indicators: the direct and indirect creation of jobs, and our CO_2 footprint. We decided to measure these indicators at the portfolio level because it would be impossible and unreasonable for investment officers to select projects based on these variables. In order to steer the organisation, we decided to set targets for green investments and for catalysing. Catalysing third party money was crucial to reaching our goals. This is one of the reasons we created FMO Investment Management Company in order to reach out to pension funds and impact investors and offer them the possibility of investing in a cross-section of FMO's portfolio.

LEADERSHIP PROGRAMME

Once we had defined our new strategy, we initiated our leadership programme which was to prepare management to lead the implementation of a more complex strategy in a fast-changing world. I had thought that everyone was aligned with our new strategy, so it came as a shock to find out at our first meeting that there were still doubts about the validity of the strategy. The leadership programme was to bring all of this turbulence out into the open so that the entire management layer would eventually come on board, which was essential. The discussions we had were key in helping people focus more on the solutions rather than the problems.

Externally, FMO needed to forge a stronger connection with its clients. To this end, we organised trips to visit our clients and to ask whether we could together work on a crucial issue that needed to be resolved. Part of the programme included staying at the homes of the micro-entrepreneurs or farmers who were the clients of our clients. For everyone involved, this was to be a stirring experience that brought us back to the essence of why we were doing what we were doing and for whom.

THE NEXT STEP

By the end of 2016, we expect to be on track to meet our 2020 target of doubling jobs and halving our carbon dioxide emissions. But even beyond 2020, I am confident that FMO will continue to evolve and improve. We are already busy studying the next metrics of environmental sustainability by which to steer the organisation. And we are experimenting with how best to define inclusive finance and the effective strategies to address it. We are searching for new products to catalyse funds through our Fund Management Company. When we embarked on our new strategy, we knew it would be a journey full of obstacles and one of trial and error –

but also one with valuable lessons. I have no doubt that FMO will continue to explore and to learn, and I hope that our learning process will be of value to others.

Looking at chapters five and six, it is not to difficult to see what the next steps in FMO's future strategy will look like. They will be linked to reaching the Global Goals by 2030, and the generations of FMO employees after me will define how to get us there.

EPILOGUE

I would like to end this book by recounting two remarkable things that happened to me which together have brought me full circle.

COMING FULL CIRCLE

A few years ago, my son informed me that he wanted to work in private equity and that he had found a job with a private equity fund in emerging markets. It was an extraordinary feeling to see him choosing to focus on an industry and a market close to my own. He was first sent to Peru, the country where my wife was born and where we first met. It was also where I did my thesis and received my first work experience. My son was then sent to Ghana, the first developing country that I had visited during my studies. It was there that I had had my AIESEC[*] traineeship with the Barclays Bank. To meet my son at a reception at the Dutch Embassy in Accra and speak to the CEO of a company that both FMO *and* my son's private equity company work with – that is truly special. Father and son were now able to share our experiences in investing in emerging markets!

And in another such extraordinary coincidence, I found myself one day reviewing an investment that FMO made in a private equity fund that finances conservation projects in the tropical rain forests of Peru (including the Cordillera Azul in San Martin) by supporting small farmers who cultivate cacao and other crops. A year later we were financing the leading chocolate company in Peru with a loan to provide their small farmer suppliers with the finance to improve their productivity. The chocolate company happens to source their cacao from San Martin, the

---

[*] AIESEC is a global organisation offering young people cross-cultural internships, leadership development, and volunteer exchange programmes.

same region where I carried out fieldwork in 1978 for my Master's thesis! The subject of my thesis was how small farmers in San Martin adopt innovation. Of course, nobody believes me when I explain that I was completely uninvolved in the sourcing of this transaction. I was amazed at how circles tend to complete themselves, eventually returning to where they began.

My main motivation for writing this book was to share both FMO's experiences and my own so that others can build on our lessons. I want to demonstrate and prove the important role that development finance institutions play in bridging the divide between the public and private sectors, enabling investments to be scaled up in the path towards a better future. I urge governments to strenghten DFIs so that we may collectively reach the Global Goals by 2030.

Finally, I want to call upon all governments, businesses, and especially financial institutions to take action and make the changeover to sustainable development. In order to stay relevant, we all need to ask ourselves: what do I see as a better world? And how can I contribute to sustainable development? By purposefully taking part in shaping the future, we can offer a better world to our children and our children's children.

ACKNOWLEDGEMENTS

There are a number of people we wish to thank wholeheartedly for their valuable contributions to our somewhat crazy undertaking – wanting to write a book as a side project next to our jobs and families and doing so in a limited amount of time.

But first we would like to remember our dear colleague and friend, Desmond Fortes, who died unexpectedly in an accident while on holiday with his friends just as we started writing this book. We believe the title of this book is in line with his spirit. We wish Femke Brouwer, his beloved wife and our colleague, and their two beautiful children, Luca and Nina, the strength and the courage to get through the days ahead.

For their input on particular parts of the text and for the useful bits of information they provided, we would like to thank Clem van den Berg, Yvonne Bakkum, Edwin van der Haar, Paul Hartogsveld, Anton Timpers, Marleen van Ruijven, Georges Beukering, Loucky Spit, Anne-Rieke Oskamp, Frederik Jan van den Bosch, Elisabeth Wegen and Varishna Tewarie.

For sharing their stories, experiences, and insights during interviews, we thank Gerhard Engel, Connor McEnroy, Mo Ibrahim, Kshama Fernandes, Aziz Mebarek, Maurits Groen, Patience Mayaki, Bas Rekvelt, Mareike Hussels, Huub Cornelissen, Emile Groot, Ben Zwinkels, Martin Steindl, and Chantal Korteweg.

The time-consuming and brave task of proofreading the text and providing us with brutally honest feedback was diligently undertaken by Hanke Lange, Heleen Tiemersma, Jorim Schraven, Pieter van der Gaag, Lisette van der Boog, and Huib-Jan de Ruijter. Without your constructive yet critical feedback, this book would not have developed as quickly as it did.

There are some people who deserve an extra special thank you. First and foremost, we wholeheartedly thank Haico Kaashoek for his youthful enthusiasm, his relentless dedication, and most importantly his knack for finding the right words; Gioia Marini for her diligent effort in making our words matter; Tom Cummings for being an inspirational and meaningful sparring partner; René de Sévaux for his valuable support in reading, commenting, planning, and doing whatever else was necessary; Anke Terlinck for organising Nanno's time so that he had enough of it to dedicate to writing; Angelica Ortiz-de Haas for her understanding and patience in allowing Marijn to spend a large portion of her time away from the team to work on this book; and Ebissé Rouw of Amsterdam University Press for believing we could make this happen and finally Léon Hulst for his careful design of the book.

Working with our FMO colleagues over these years has been fantastic and a lot of fun. We have shared innumerable beautiful experiences. All our FMO colleagues have been an inspiration for this book. Thank you all!

Last but not least, our respective partners Mirian Garcia and Antoś Szkudlarek deserve our deep gratitude for bearing with us in all our crazy undertakings. We are certain they will be both proud and relieved once this book is published. Thank you for your love and your patience.

ACRONYM GLOSSARY

AIESEC   *Association internationale des étudiants en sciences économiques et commerciales*, the largest global network of students

CABEI   Central American Bank for Economic Integration

COPINH Council of Indigenous Peoples of Honduras

COP21   Conference of Parties, 21, also known as the 2015 Paris Climate Conference

DFI   Development Finance Institution

FMO   *Financierings-Maatschappij voor Ontwikkelingslanden*, Netherlands Development Finance Company

FPIC   Free, Prior, and Informed Consent

GABV   Global Alliance for Banking on Value

GDP   Gross Domestic Product

GIIN   Global Impact Investment Network

IFC   International Finance Corporation

IFHA   Investment Fund for Healthcare in Africa

IMF   International Monetary Fund

IRIS   Impact Reporting and Investment Standards

MCF   Medical Credit Fund

MDG   Millennium Development Goal

MIT   Massachusetts Institute of Technology

NGO   non-governmental organisation

ODA   official development aid

OECD   Organisation for Economic Co-operation and Development

SDG   Sustainable Development Goal

SME   small and medium-sized enterprises

USAID   United States Agency for International Development

WBCSD World Business Council for Sustainable Development

REFERENCES

Runde, Daniel F.; Moser, Helen. July 2015. "DFI Finance Increases to One Half of ODA." Center for Strategic International Studies. Washington, D.C. <http://csis.org/ publication/dfi-finance-increases-one-half-oda>

World Business Council for Sustainable Development. 2010. *Vision 2050: The New Agenda for Business*. WBCSD. <http://www.wbcsd.org/WEB/PROJECTS/BZROLE/VISION 2050-FULLREPORT_FINAL.PDF>

United Nations. October 1970. *International Development Strategy for the Second United Nations Development Decade, UN General Assembly Resolution 2626 (XXV)*. United Nations. A/RES/25/2626.<http://www.un-documents.net/a25r2626.htm>

OECD. 2016. *Net ODA: Total, % of gross national income, 2000 – 2014*. Net ODA (indicator). doi: 10.1787/33346549-en. <https://data.oecd.org/oda/net-oda.htm>

United Nations Secretary General. September 2001. *Road map towards the implementation of the United Nations Millennium Declaration*. United Nations. A/56/326. <http://www.un.org/documents/ga/docs/56/a56326.pdf>

United Nations Economic Commission for Africa, African Union, African Development Bank and United Nations Development Programme. September 2015. *MDG Report 2015: Assessing Progress in Africa toward the Millennium Development Goals*. United Nations. Addis Ababa, Ethiopia. <http://www.undp.org/content/dam/rba/docs/Reports/MDG_Africa_Report_2014_ENG.pdf>

United Nations Economic, Scientific, and Cultural Organization. 2015. *Education for All 2000-2015: Achievements and Challenges*. UNESCO. Paris, France. <http://unesdoc.unesco.org/images/0023/002322/232205e.pdf>

Sumner, Andy. June 2012. *Where Do The World's Poor Live?: A New Update*. Institute of Development Studies Working Paper. Volume 2012, No. 393. <https://www.ids.ac.uk/files/dmfile/Wp393.pdf>

See Sustainable Development Goals Official Website: <https://sustainabledevelopment.un.org/?menu=1300>

UNFCCC. December 2015. *Adoption of the Paris Agreement*. United Nations. FCCC/CP/2015/L.9/Rev.1, 12. <https://unfccc.int/resource/docs/2015/cop21/eng/ l09r01.pdf>

See Green Climate Fund Pledge Tracker Website: <http://www.greenclimate.fund/contributions/pledge-tracker>

United Nations. 2014. *The Millennium Development Goals Report 2014*. United

Nations. New York. 2014.
<http://www.un.org/millenniumgoals/2014%20MDG%20report/
MDG%202014%20English%20web.pdf>

Olinto, Pedro; Beegle, Kathleen; Sobrado, Carlos; Uematsu, Hiroki. October 2013 *The State of the Poor: Where Are The Poor, Where Is Extreme Poverty Harder to End, and What Is the Current Profile of the World's Poor?* The World Bank. Number 125.
<http://siteresources.worldbank.org/EXTPREMNET/Resources/EP125.pdf>

Ferreira, Francisco H. G.; Chen, Shaohua; Dabalen, Andrew L.; Dikhanov, Yuri M.; Hamadeh, Nada; Jolliffe, Dean Mitchell; Narayan, Ambar; Prydz, Espen Beer; Revenga, Ana L.; Sangraula, Prem; Serajuddin, Umar; Yoshida, Nobuo. 2015. *A global count of the extreme poor in 2012: data issues, methodology and initial results.* World Bank Group. Policy Research working paper; no. WPS 7432. Washington, D.C.
<http://documents.worldbank.org/curated/en/2015/10/25114899/global-count-extreme-poor-2012-data-issues-methodology-initial-results>

United Nations, Department of Economic and Social Affairs, Population Division. 2015. *World Population Prospects: The 2015 Revision*, custom data acquired via website.
<http://esa.un.org/unpd/wpp/DataQuery/>

United Nations Department of Economic and Social Affairs, Population Division. 2015. *World Population Prospects: The 2015 Revision, Key Findings and Advance Tables.* United Nations. ESA/P/WP.241. New York.
<http://esa.un.org/unpd/wpp/publications/files/ key_findings_wpp_2015.pdf>

Dabla-Norris, Era; Kochhar, Kalpana; Suphaphiphat, Nujin; Ricka, Frantisek;

Tsounta, Evridiki. June 2015. *Causes and Consequences of Income Inequality: A Global Perspective.* International Monetary Fund. SDN/15/13.
<https://www.imf.org/external/pubs/ft/sdn/2015/sdn1513.pdf>

Christian Gonzales, Sonali Jain-Chandra, Kalpana Kochhar, Monique Newiak, and Tlek Zeinullayev. October 2015. *Catalyst for Change: Empowering Women and Tackling Income Inequality.* International Monetary Fund. SDN/15/20.
<https://www.imf.org/external/pubs/ft/sdn/2015/sdn1520.pdf>

IFC. January 2013. *IFC Jobs Study: Assessing Private Sector Contributions to Job Creation and Poverty Reduction.* International Finance Corporation. Washington, D.C.
<http://www.ifc.org/wps/wcm/connect/0fe6e2804e2c0a8f8d3bad7a9dd66321/IFC_FULL+JOB+STUDY+REPORT_JAN2013_FINAL.pdf?MOD=AJPERES>

World Business Council for Sustainable Development. 2010. *Vision 2050: The New Agenda for Business.* WBCSD.
<http://www.wbcsd.org/WEB/PROJECTS/BZROLE/ VISION2050-FULLREPORT_FINAL.PDF>

El Idrissi, Ali; Saltuk, Yasemin; Bouri, Amit; Mudaliar, Abhilash; Schiff, Hannah. May 2015. *Eyes on the Horizon: The Impact Investor Survey.* J.P. Morgan and the Global Impact Investing Network.
<https://thegiin.org/assets/documents/pub/2015.04%20Eyes%20on%20the%20Horizon.pdf>
Leijonhufvud, Christina; O'Donohoe, Nick; Saltuk, Yasemin; Bugg-Levine, Antony; Brandenburg, Margot. November 2010. *Impact Investments: An Emerging Asset Class.* J.P. Morgan, Rockefeller Foundation, and the Global Impact

Investing Network. <https://thegiin.org/assets/documents/Impact%20Investments%20an%20Emerging%20Asset%20Class2.pdf>

International Energy Agency. 2015. *Energy and Climate Change: World Energy Outlook Special Report*. International Energy Agency, OECD. <https://www.iea.org/publications/freepublications/publication/WEO2015SpecialReportonEnergyandClimateChange.pdf>

United Nations Conference on Trade and Development (Division on Investment and Enterprise). 2014. *World Investment Report 2014: Investing in the SDGs: An Action Plan*. UNCTD. <http://unctad.org/en/PublicationsLibrary/wir2014_en.pdf>

Schmidt-Traub, Guido. November 201. *Investment Needs to Achieve the Sustainable Development Goals*. Sustainable Development Solutions Network. <http://unsdsn.org/wp-content/uploads/2015/09/151112-SDG-Financing-Needs.pdf>

The Financial System We Need: Aligning the Financial System with Sustainability. October 2015, UNEP. http://apps.unep.org/publications/index.php?option=com_pub&task=download&file=011830_en

de Martelaere, Patricia. *Taoisme: De weg om niet te volgen*. Amsterdam: Ambo Anthos, 2007.

Heider, John. *De Tao van het leiderschap: Strategieen voor de nieuwe tijd*. Amsterdam: Contact, 1995.

van Lommel, Pim. *Eindeloos bewustzijn*. Utrecht: Uitgeverij Ten Have, 2007.

See the Natural Capital Protocol on the Official Natural Capital Coalition Website: <http://www.naturalcapitalcoalition.org/natural-capital-protocol.html> See the Official EDFI Association Website: <http://www.edfi.be/>

Blended Finance: Trending Blending – the fad for mixing public, charitable and private money, April 2016, The Economist

Redesigning Development Finance Initiatives – Blended finance: A primer for development finance and philanthropic funders, September 2015, OECD and WEF

How Gender Equality can boost Economic Growth, October 2013, by DEVEX editor, DEVEX